TELEPHONE COLLECTION
Domestic & International Solutions

*The moneylender
has a better memory
than the debtor does*

Benjamin Franklin

TELEPHONE COLLECTION
Domestic & International Solutions

EMILE VAN VEEN

ERIC A. MACDONALD

Increase your efficiency! Telephone demands are 80 percent more effective than letters and faxes.

Tips, guidelines and techniques to improve the payment practices of your customers while enhancing your service!

Telephone Collection: Domestic & International Solutions
Van Veen, Emile F.
MacDonald, Eric A.
Graydon Group
Amsterdam
ISBN 90 75348 21 5
NUGI 684
Keywords: collection – debtors – by telephone – telephone techniques

Photo sleeve: © Zefa Nederland B.V.

© E.F. van Veen/1998
Eric A. MacDonald/1998

Printed: Hofstad Druktechniek, Zoetermeer

CONTENTS

———

INTRODUCTION

The check is in the mail....

Is the check ever really in the mail? Chances are if you're calling the debtor, the check is nowhere near the post office.

Moreover, mañana is not a tropical drink! Being told that you will be paid "mañana" (tomorrow) has become a time-honored tradition for putting off payment indefinitely on any outstanding receivables.

This book addresses communications techniques that can be used for effective collections calls and provides some helpful hints on the domestic and international fronts for establishing credit procedure. For those readers starting their careers in credit, you will find useful and practical approaches to account management and collections. Experienced credit executives will benefit from this publication through reminders of what they may already know and by adding to their existing knowledge with some of the tips provided in the pages that follow.

Slow payments are endemic to trade whether it is domestic or international. The slow payment practice is much more than a mere annoyance; it can generate enormous costs to the company extending credit. An invoice that is paid 30 days late costs a company with an average profit margin, at least 2 percent of the profit on the transaction. Companies do not go bankrupt through a lack of turnover, but through a lack of capital or poor cash flow!

Written demands have proven to produce only meager results when it comes to collections especially if these are overseas. Their effectiveness is aided if legal intervention is sought but, in general, letters written by an average creditor to a debtor do not produce the desired effect. Telephone collection is therefore the weapon of choice against the slow or non-paying customer, but the manner in which we use that weapon can always be improved.

How can you distinguish yourself from all the other telephone credit managers and collectors in order to produce positive results? How do you ensure that your point of view comes across as original, efficient, commercially friendly and how do you communicate that you must be paid now, while ensuring that your customer will adhere to agreements in the future?

Those are the questions, which we will address and answer in this book. Credit management is much more than administering and monitoring outstanding debts. The modern business environment continuously demands a more personal approach, from the inception of the service that is provided to the customer to the moment when it should be indicated that this service wasn't provided free of charge and has to be paid for!

Evaporating Standards
In the last few years, there has been more and more talk of the lack of standards relating to the payment of bills. Modern credit managers who want to operate efficiently, can no longer confine themselves to merely sending out second, third, fourth, fifth and "final" payment notices. They must seek personal contact with the customer and reach the objective by means of direct confrontation.

An objective which should not only of collecting the debt, as every contact with a customer is by definition a commercial contact, but offer many more possibilities and opportunities for contact, new sales and a growing future relationship.

How to accomplish the above objectives through a defined strategy will be reviewed in this book, along with methods of responding to a customer's "counter-arguments" or excuses. Every credit manager knows how inventive debtors can be in making up pretexts and excuses – but what constitutes a fictional best seller and what is a viable and acceptable excuse? How can these two be separated and how should you best approach the debtor's line of reasoning as they present to you their version of the facts?

A variety of different options will be discussed with clear examples and tips, so that after reading this book you will be able to enter into a productive discussion with your debtor armed with a number of useful and effective "tools".

Communication
"Communication" is one of the key concepts explored in the book. Communication and discussion are the resources with which the credit manager is equipped to achieve his or her objective. Although communication as a general concept is fairly pervasive throughout the manual, in one form or another, it is worthwhile to consciously pause and consider the method in which we go about the business of communicating.

By consciously determining the structure of a conversation, choosing the correct words and inflection and *listening* more closely, better and quicker results can clearly be achieved. Not only results pertaining to the payment of invoices but those that are inherent in the impression that is left with the customer for future commercial contact.

Communication by telephone remains slightly more awkward than a "face-to-face" conversation. Without the possibility of transmitting or receiving body language, everything boils down to the extent to which the conversation partners know how to make use of their telephone techniques and the words and inflection that they will employ during the course of a verbal exchange. You will soon notice that using the right tone, emphasizing the correct word in a sentence and the use of precise and conscious pauses can actually deliver amazing results.......

Why is good credit management so important?
In many companies " outstanding accounts receivable" remain a conspicuous item when undertaking budget planning. Whereas sizeable investments are made in marketing and sales, (too) little attention has historically been paid to post-sales administration.

The financial impact of good credit management is much greater than many corporate leaders are willing to admit. In the Netherlands, for example, the average invoice is still paid approximately 26 days late. In some countries that number escalates from 60 to 90 days before a debt is collected. Nevertheless, poor country or industry average payment performance should never form grounds for accepting the same from your own customers. Instead, using the averages should help to plan around suspected late payers. The costs of unpaid debts are considerably high, and it should never be your company's intention to act as a "bank" for its customers.

In a recent survey performed by Graydon (1997) using a sample of 5,600 bankruptcies, more than 30 percent of these defaults were caused by non or slow paying customers.

A lack of cash flow, not a lack of sales or turnover is the number one reason for bankruptcy!

How much misery can be avoided through proper and informed credit management? Why should people simply accept that someone not meet their previous commitments? You have, after all, ensured that you met your commitments with regard to the time of delivery? How would the customer have reacted if *you* had delivered "just" a month too late?

Payment for goods and services is just as much a concrete part of a business contract as the delivery. Your customer must be reminded and committed to the terms of the agreement.

Sold is only when paid ...

10

"Right away" is easily said
(Shakespeare)

1. COMMUNICATION

Com•mu•ni•ca•tion [-(t)sion] (*<Fr<Lat*) *n* (-s) 1 announcement, notification; 2 giving or exchanging information, knowledge, messages etc..

Com•mu•ni•cate (*<Lat*) (communicating, past part. communicated) 1 to announce, to notify of; 2 people in contact with each other; 3 to exchange information, to be in spiritual contact with each other: *with someone.*

We do it every day and all day, consciously, but probably more often unconsciously. Sometimes successfully, other times with varying degrees of success and control.

In our modern society, communication is becoming *the* magic word for success. Everyone must be able to communicate with everyone else as instantaneously as possible and maximum accessibility has become an absolute must.

Compared to roughly a hundred years ago, the world has changed a hundred times. Of revolutionary significance in the world of communication was the invention of the telephone. This instrument rapidly expanded from local access to international connections. In the last fifteen years one medium after the next has appeared. The telex was quickly followed by the fax, which then rapidly lost ground to "e-mail". In the Netherlands, for example, there are currently already more than a million mobile telephones in use, and even more so in the United States. These mobiles belong to people who want to be continuously available. For those who are momentarily not in a position to answer their telephone, messages can nevertheless still be received via "voice mail"; on the mobile, at the office or simply at home.

Coupled with this instant access, the possibilities of meeting people in person have only improved. Every place on earth can be reached within 20 hours, and most people have car at their disposal for shorter distances? Soon the videophone will enable you to look at the person you are talking to. Until that innovation becomes common place, you will still need your phone techniques.

With all of this technology at our disposal, are we *better* able to communicate with each other? The answer to this question is regrettably an emphatic "no". We are *more frequently* in contact with each other, but it may be precisely for this very reason that we are probably less effective.....

Conscious and Unconscious, Verbal and Non-verbal Communication

Although people probably do not realize it, very often our lives are one long sequence of communicative events; most of which occur at an unconscious level. Brief contacts with people who we do not know which constitute contact and communication nonetheless.

Communication begins when we get up in the morning and speak to our partner, and possibly the other members of our family. Sure, some of it might be characterized as non-verbal grunting but it is communication. Later, when we set out to drive to work, we communicate with other drivers: some people will tailgate a "dawdler", clearly making their message known.

Walking along the street and making eye contact with someone is communicating, just as stepping aside for someone is also a form of communication. All of this happens almost unconsciously, but in this manner we are all basically in continuous communication contact with our fellow man.

Communication, therefore, does not necessarily have to be verbal, and in many cases it occurs non-verbally. Non-verbal communication plays a very important role during verbal contact (spoken conversation).

For example, the manner in which we sit, watch, or move our hands are all indications of how we feel and what we are trying to express which sends out a message to the conversation partner. It is not surprising that we can sometimes see, in just a blink of an eye, whether someone is in a bad mood or is perhaps nervous or uncertain. Sometimes, the signals are clearer than at other times, and in many cases we can use these signals to our advantage.

On the other hand, we can also use our body to clarify words and emphasize them. We demonstrate points with hand and arm movements, we frown when we hear bad news and we smile when we hear good news. But we also smile to make a friendly impression, to put someone at ease or to even try to soften the blow when delivering an unpleasant message.

Nuances: The manner in which things are said

In a normal conversation, both verbal and non-verbal messages play a role. The spoken message is highly dependent on the manner in which it is expressed, the inflection.

We convey what we mean through the manner in which we say something, although the content of the actual conversation may be completely the opposite. If it is raining heavily, we may sarcastically say: "Lovely weather isn't it?" To the recipient of the message, it is nevertheless clear that we actually mean that the weather is awful. The ability to recognize word play is often dependent on someone's mastery of the language. Someone unfamiliar with English, in this example, might actually think that the weather is awful or that the speaker is in need of medication.

By emphasizing certain words, the actual meaning of a sentence can be changed completely. The examples below demonstrate this very clearly:

A couple is sitting at a restaurant terrace. The man says to his wife:

"This is very nice, isn't it?"

But what does he actually mean?

"This (the food) is very nice, isn't it?"

"This (the atmosphere) is very nice, isn't it!?"

The meaning can also be completely reversed by changing the tone and stressing a different word:

Oh, this is *nice*! Meaning what a disgusting shame.

The concept of "communication" can be reduced to a single premise: conveying a message from a sender to a receiver.

The sender transmits the message that is then picked up by the receiver. The receiver must first decipher the message and ask themselves what do these words mean? Moreover, what do these words mean in combination with any specific non-verbal communication and in context.

Frame of reference
As a rule, talking to someone we know well creates very few problems in terms of misunderstandings. They already have some frame of reference from their experience concerning how certain of our expressions are intended, which facial aspect belongs to which mood. Two colleagues who have been working with each other in the same room for years can know what is meant by a single word.

On the other hand, if we have to deal with someone completely unknown, certain unexpected problems can arise. Two people, for example, make a deal, where one person promises to *"send the credit transfer to the bank at the first opportunity"*. The other will probably expect the money in the account within a week. In the debtor's company, however, all bills are only paid once a month, so it is possible that payment will take three weeks.

It is important to be aware of the conversation partner's circumstances and context. You cannot simply say to someone: 'Isn't it great, Liverpool beat Manchester United 4-1!' One person may smile in glee; the other may well not be able to appreciate such a statement. Remember that references to national pass-times in an international context often fall flat. Many Americans reading this sentence may wonder who on earth Liverpool is meant to be and if they are a sports team, what are they playing?

If you talk about *"red"* with an accountant and an electrician you will get two diametrically opposed perceptions. The accountant, when hearing the color, will associate it with negative or loss, but the electrician will associate the color red with positive or plus.

A message is therefore "deciphered" by each person in a different manner. When hearing certain words or concepts, associations are summoned that are not always easy to predict. It is important to accustom ourselves to the "perceptions" of a conversation partner. If we know little or nothing about them, it is advisable to choose our words very carefully and to make extra checks so that the message has been adequately conveyed and interpreted in the manner intended.

These "perceptions" can be clarified with the "frame of reference" concept. The frame of reference is formed over the years, by things such as upbringing, education, intelligence, character, personal standards and values, experiences and expectations.

The content of a conversation is not only determined by the words we express, but by the interaction of a number of factors. Those factors can be split up into two categories; non-verbal and verbal:

16

Non-verbal
– Atmosphere
– Surroundings
– Posture
– Gestures
– Eye contact

Verbal
– Inflection
– Stress
– Word choice
– Message

We will now briefly discuss each of the verbal and non-verbal aspects of communication between people. The non-verbal communication cannot be used as a tool in a telephone call, but we will show you some very efficient and helpful words, sentences and ways to substitute those factors; making the non-verbal, verbal!

Atmosphere
Every conversation has a certain atmosphere; formal, relaxed, serious, friendly, hostile, etc. The atmosphere in which a conversation proceeds can partially determine to what extent a conversation partner is receptive, feels at ease and participates.

Surroundings
The surroundings in which you have a conversation are very important. A conversation in the pub is much less likely to falter than a conversation at the office. The appearance of an office is also important; someone with a nicely furnished and presentable office will be taken more seriously than someone with a shabby and filthy, disorganized working environment.

In addition, influences from the surroundings can strongly affect a conversation; loud music, rattling type machines, construction work, but also poor or unflattering light are factors that can be distracting and can negatively impact upon a conversation.

Posture

Physical attitude during a conversation is very important for communication. The way in which we hold our bodies gives off very clear signals – interested, disinterested, nonchalant, confident, nervous, distant, open, asleep etc.

Our conversation partner reacts unconsciously to these non-verbal cues. If, for example, someone gets the impression that they are talking to an uninterested person, they will try to make a greater impression by talking loudly and making gestures.

Gestures

Using body movements, mostly our hands, arms and head, we try to increase the impact of our words or clarify them. Interestingly, the amount of gestures used in a conversation varies significantly with different cultures. In Southern Europe the gesture is king. Sometimes it appears to supersede the actual verbal communication. Contrariwise, in Japan, gestures are minimal; arms are kept tightly to the side if two colleagues meet. In the United States, anchormen on TV have been told to sit on their hands to avoid too much gesticulation.

Everyone uses gestures, but the gestures that we make are not so universal that everyone understands what is being indicated by our body language. In fact, many gestures that we take for granted in our culture as acceptable; often have rude and insulting meanings in other cultures. Something to take into account when face to face communication occurs.

Gestures are enormously important for communication. By nodding confirmation we indicate that we have understood something, by frowning or shrugging our shoulders we indicate that the opposite is true. Gestures also effect the atmosphere of a conversation. We can clearly demonstrate with our bodies, for example, that it is good to see someone (smile, slap on the shoulders, waving). Again, some degree of skepticism is needed when you are communicating with customers from other countries. Your Japanese business partner, for instance, may nod and nod and not have agreed with or understood a thing you have said.

The telephone is a powerful weapon
(M.D.J. Schols)

Eye contact

By looking someone in the eye we are clearly making very personal contact. It is the number one method for holding the attention of a conversation partner in the Western world.

The eye has been described as "the mirror of the soul". Far more often than we realize, our eyes reveal whether we are happy, sad, observant, tired or healthy. No less than 15 small muscles surround our eyes and determine the position of the eyes, eyelids and eyebrows. It is not surprising that the eye can have many different "looks", and that nervous twitches almost always first manifest themselves around the eyes.

Eye contact in a conversation is an important medium of communication. By looking someone straight in the eye, we allow them a glimpse into our souls, which conveys a signal of honesty and sincerity.

Again, eye-to-eye contact in some cultures is considered rude and a sign of disrespect. Always be aware of your surroundings and of values that may be dissimilar to your own.

Inflection

The tone in which we speak represents an important aspect of a conversation. People speak differently to a seven year-old child than to an adult.

'Don't talk to me in that tone of voice!' is protest against the perceived negative manner adopted by the speaker, but there is a great deal more to impart by the way in which we speak. Anger, nervousness, joy..... are all emotions that we express vocally.

Many people will increase the volume of their voices if they have the feeling that their message is not coming across very well, or if they do not have the undivided attention of their conversation partner. In such an instance, why not try speaking softly; you will be amazed at the effects. By speaking more softly we are slightly less understandable, forcing the conversation partner to listen closely and to shut off distracting external influences.

Raising your voice can be a good weapon, but only when used sparingly. By using a consistent and balanced conversational tone, a sudden raised voice can produce a real shock effect. This should be managed very carefully, because there is a significant chance that the signal produced as a result of the increase in volume may be read as hostile. This may mean, "the tone has been irrevocably set..."

Stress
By stressing certain words, we emphasize their importance. Through the proper use of stress in sentences we not only speak more clearly, but also in a more lively and animated manner.

Place stress as much as possible on words that have actual reference to the content of the message to be communicated, so that maximum efficiency is achieved. Misplaced stress, as seen in the previous examples, can sometimes completely change the meaning of a sentence.

Word choice
It seems obvious that we should choose the clearest words to effectively communicate. However it is not that simple. Since everyone has a different frame of reference, not all words are equally suitable for everyone. Acronyms and industry terms are especially confusing in a credit-related conversation or in any conversation for that matter when both parties do not have the same frame of reference.

Is your DSO similar to NACM industry standards in ASEAN countries?

In the example above, the speaker is asking whether your days-sales outstanding is similar to that of the National Association of Credit Manager's industry statistics in countries that are members of the Association of South East Asian Nations.

The original question presupposes a significant amount of knowledge that you must ascertain is held by your conversation partner prior to the conversation taking place. Otherwise, utilizing technical jargon can not only be confusing but it can make the other party uncomfortable or embarrassed to ask about a term that it appears should be a familiar one.

There are so many options for phrasing a message, and a choice of synonyms exists for almost every word there is. A 26-year window cleaner would be approached in a different manner than a 63-year-old lawyer; the latter might be more comfortable with what we term the ten-dollar words.

By consciously managing these differences, by tuning ourselves into our conversation partner's frame of reference, we can acquire the knowledge to better and more efficiently communicate.

Message

The message is actually what it's all about; the objective of the conversation. What do we actually want to precisely convey to our conversation partner? That message, which is clear to us, must be sent out as effectively as possible. The content is conveyed with the aid of the above-mentioned communication methods.

All these factors together determine the success or failure of a conversation. Research has shown that non-verbal factors are more important than verbal factors, determining at least 55% of the quality of a conversation.

Non-verbal
- Atmosphere
- Surroundings
- Posture   *55%*
- Gestures
- Eye contact

Verbal
- Inflection
- Stress   *45%*
- Word choice
- Message

If we now relate this knowledge to a telephone conversation, it is immediately clear that we are seriously handicapped in comparison to a face-to-face conversation. After all, in a telephone conversation we only have 45 percent of the aids that determine the success of a conversation at our disposal.

During the course of a telephone conversation, the extent to which we are used to talking with expressions seems all too obvious. Almost everyone uses hand and arm gestures on the telephone, nods approvingly, or shakes their head and smiles... as if the person on the other end of the line could see us.

Not only does this look a little odd, the danger here is that because we think we have, for example, nodded in agreement that we do not subsequently communicate our assent clearly enough. In a face-to-face conversation a great deal of the gestures and signals *replace* words, you do not have this arsenal of body language at you disposal on the telephone. How do you overcome this obstacle?

Effect through the telephone

As a telephone conversation simply does not offer the options of a face-to-face conversation, we must consciously compensate for the function of signals with certain words. This, in turn, can create the possibility of generating some atmosphere, thereby making the contact more personal. Several tips are provided below for replacing non-verbal communication with words.

Atmosphere

As a rule, we convey a feeling of friendliness or trust with our visual expression. Take the trouble in a telephone conversation to say that you are pleased that someone called, since on the other end of the line your joyous smile remains quite invisible.

Consciously say something about the emotion you wish to convey. Calmly state whether you are disappointed, angry or satisfied. This establishes clarity, creates an atmosphere and points the conversation much more purposefully in the direction in which you want it to go.

"Ah, Mr. Williams, I am pleased that you called! I wanted to tell you how appreciative I was that you transferred the amount directly into our account as agreed!"

Surroundings

Since no one can simply look down the telephone wire (well not yet in most offices), it is fairly difficult to convey something about your

24

surroundings. It is nevertheless very useful to convey an impression by means of words. For example, in the sentence: "I have the items lying here in front of me on my desk," you are conveying an interested and businesslike impression.

By saying something about yourself and your surroundings, even though this has absolutely no relevance to the content, you can break the ice and improve your chances of catching the other person's attention. 'I'm just walking round my desk!' seems a completely pointless remark, but it means that at that moment your conversation partner "visualizes" how you are doing that, and as a result, they are more involved with you and with the conversation.

"One moment, I'm just getting it. I've just been trying to get through the mail that's piled up, so there's not a square inch left on my desk. Just a second, I'll clear some space!"

Posture
Our posture is more difficult to convey, but it is really important to assume an active and interested attitude while having a telephone conversation. Sitting up with good posture can produce remarkable effects on clarity of thought and expression.

A great many postures can be reproduced with words, but they do have to be consciously spoken. Short sentences such as 'I'm on the edge of my seat', 'I'm completely bowled over!' or 'I'm going to have to sit up straight for this!' indicate your expression of interest and your posture. Your conversation partner will be able to visualize such an expression directly while you will have succeeded in conveying a signal.

"I'm all ears!"
"I'm completely bowled over!"
"My eyes almost popped out of their sockets!"
"I just can't wait!"
"I'm on pins and needles"

The smile on your face will be expressed in your voice, your smile can be heard in your tone!

Gestures
We use gestures to indicate or clarify something. Instead of nodding in agreement when discussing an issue with your conversation partner, you can indicate that you are listening to them and that you are in agreement using only short words. The inclination to constantly use the word "yes" is fine, but it is by interchanging the use of alternatives such as "right", "agreed", "indeed", "really?" or "of course" that much more effect is achieved. In fact, varying these expressions is advised. Sometimes, after having heard the word "right" thirty times during the course of a conversation, you get the impression that no one is listening and that things aren't quite *"right"*.

We normally make use of gestures to add impact or clarify our words; on the telephone we must choose our words, inflections and stress with extra care. This is not always simple, but by paying particular attention to your choice of expressions during a telephone conversation you can succeed in training yourself:

During a telephone conversation, you unwittingly use a number of gestures. Pay attention to *when* you do this, and in such cases take the time to check whether you were clearly understood. It is likely that you will unconsciously trust the explanatory action of such a gesture.

By doing this consistently, you will start to notice that you use accents and stresses much more purposefully. Subsequently check whether your message has now been communicated as intended at the correct moment.

Eye contact

Eye contact represents the most personal part of a conversation. In telephone discussions it can be partially replaced by regularly saying and repeating the name of the conversation partner. In that manner you are talking to them directly, which in turn guarantees that their attention is that much more heightened.

"With all due respect Mr. Williams, that really isn't acceptable to us..."
"Of course Mr. Williams, but..."

It is not advisable to overuse this technique which can quickly become irritating to the listener. "That's my name don't wear it out."

Used in small doses, particularly just before an extra important piece of information or denial, it can deliver extremely good results.

Listening and pauses

Now that we have talked extensively about active communication in the context of a conversation, "passive" communication must also be explored in order to complete the communication process.

By passive communication we mean communication in which we are recipients of information and *don't* speak; in other words **listening** and the use of **pauses**. The receiving of information.

Listening, in particular, is a part of the technique of conversation that the overwhelming majority of people have yet to master? We are all too quickly inclined to interrupt the conversation partner in order to take control of the conversation. This habit is not only exceptionally irritating, but it is also the cause of much miscommunication.

The most prevalent reasons why we interrupt our conversation partners are:

• because we think we know what they are going to say;
• because we think they are "reasoning incorrectly";
• because we think we have been misunderstood;
• because we do no want to hear what they are saying;
• because we think we are more important.

Strangely enough, people think that it is important that other people listen very carefully to what they have to say, and yet most of us have trouble reciprocating this same courtesy to others. The biggest problem is simply that people think four times faster than they can talk; the temptation to apply the conversational tempo to the thought tempo is often immense. We presume to already know what somebody is going to say on the basis of a few words and we finish their sentences or interrupt them to continue with our own story.

Herein lies the danger; namely because it is often the case that someone wanted to say something *else*, a message that, by virtue of the interruption, could not be expressed or heard in full. The moment two people start talking simultaneously; neither of them will understand the other!

The propensity to reach a conclusion on the basis of half a sentence often causes us to shut ourselves off from the rest of the message. At that moment in time, we have already switched gears from receiving a message to delivering one (i.e. thinking about our answer or about the next topic).

Allowing the conversation partner to express themselves, and continuing to listen to their entire message, is therefore exceptionally important. Not only because important information may be lost, but also because that habit of cutting someone off, especially in a business contest, is perceived by most people as being extremely irritating. People have the feeling that they are not being listened to (which is true) and that they are not considered to be important. The practice of interrupting someone transcends both the message and the person being interrupted.

Good listening skills are extremely important with telephone communication; the spoken word is the only tool that is at our disposal in a telephone conversation context. Other non-verbal aids are notably absent, so the risk of miscommunication is considerably greater.

The use of pauses
Listening, or to put less delicately: not speaking, can also be an important and effective instrument in steering a conversation in another direction. In essence, the effective use of *pauses*.

In order to evaluate the correct use of pauses, it is beneficial to consider the structure of a (telephone) conversation. Every conversation consists of the interaction of (at least) two people. In turn, those people speak one or more sentences, following which the initiative is then handed over to the other. On the basis of experience, we usually know exactly when it is "our turn" to say something. From the tone of the last sentence, the message content or the silence on the other end, we realize when it is up to us to respond.

In many cultures this manner of speaking is so ingrained that we react automatically and never pause. For Native Americans, however, pauses are frequent, as are silences. It is felt that if you have nothing to say you need not fill the empty air with persiflage or banter.

On the other hand, because "conditioned behavior" does exist, becoming conscious of how the behavior manifests itself can be a useful tool that can be turned to our advantage.

If, for example, you are having a telephone conversation with someone at a company that has a mid-sized unpaid account who, in your opinion, is telling an unsatisfactory explanation, this method can be put to use with positive results. By saying absolutely nothing at the end of their story, according to the usual rules of conversation, a signal is sent out that you think that your conversation partner has not yet finished. In turn, the other party feels obliged to add to their tale, which causes them to deviate from the original plan. It is through this deviation that you will be able to detect inconsistencies, hesitation and possible discomfort.

In most cases, people are usually anxious of silences in a conversation and will try to fill in the gap by continuing to talk. You will notice that your conversation partner will carry on talking less assuredly and will perhaps even stumble over their words. They have, after all, left the safe ground of the prepared message, have already said what they wanted/were allowed to say and suddenly are forced to continue by your silence.

Consider the following:

"The problem is that we don't have any money at the moment!"
"................PAUSE................"

"You see.....,it's all pretty tight here."
"................PAUSE................"

"Investments and so forth......Customers that don't pay...... You understand, don't you?"
"................PAUSE................"

"Ah...... well, we do have SOMETHING of course......"

"Ah, so we can make some kind of agreement to reach a solution. What do you propose?"

Through the use of a pause or a silence, without actually having expressly said it, the signal is conveyed that the message was unsatisfactory. That will almost always give the receiver of that signal an uncertain feeling, which clearly shifts the balance of power in the conversation.

By allowing for a short pause, added impact can be given to an extra important message or loaded word:

"Well Mr. Williams, if we don't receive your payment by the end of the week........., I will have to take other measures."

Open-ended and closed questions
The object of a conversation is to exchange information. The effectiveness of that exchange depends on many factors, but the manner of asking questions is perhaps the most important.

Asking questions is possible in just two ways: open-ended questions or closed questions. The characteristic of closed questions is that these are designed to produce a "yes" or "no" answer, while open-ended questions require more elaboration.

30

Open-ended questions mostly begin with the letters *"H" or "W"*:

Question: *What type of assets do you have?*
Answer: *We have real property, some licenses and goodwill.*

Question: *How is it that the invoice has not been paid yet?*
Answer: *Because I haven't looked at it yet.*

Closed questions always begin with a *verb*:

Question: *Do you have everything with you?*
Answer: *Yes*

Question: *Did you pay the invoice?*
Answer: *No*

Open-ended questions yield more information and are more effective if you are on a fact-finding mission. Closed questions often compel a follow up question: Have you already paid the invoice? No ➜ Why not?

Closed questions can be used to steer conversations, get admissions, or put words in somebody's mouth: Didn't you think the meal I cooked was really enjoyable? ➜ Yes

It will not often be the case that someone will dare to answer "No" to the above question. We call this a "closed suggestive question". These types of questions can be used very effectively to elicit an answer, for example:

Question: *Don't you also think that the invoice has remained open*
              for far too long?
Answer: *Yes, you're quite right......*

By asking this type of question you are directing a response that may not necessarily always be in agreement with the actual opinion of the other......

The advantages and disadvantages of open-ended and closed questions are given below:

Advantages of open-ended questions:
• Provide detailed information
• Involve the other in the conversation
• Often provide additional data that was not asked- allow discovery of new facts
• Provide insight into opinions and feeling

Disadvantages of open-ended questions:
• Conversation can dwindle
• Less control
• Often provide additional information that you did not ask for
• The initiative can be lost

Advantages of closed questions:
• Possible to check significant amounts of data in a short time
• Strong control
• Influence through posing suggestive questions
• Can get admissions

Disadvantages of closed questions:
• Often provide little information
• Conversation partners rarely open up
• Conversation can seem like a "cross-examination"
• Through strong control some important matters are overlooked

Using closed questions is especially useful, however, with international accounts. It will direct the conversation and will allow you to get a definitive answer without taxing the linguistic ability of the other party.

Conclusion
Communication is a complex interaction of many factors. A great deal can go wrong in any communication event. While much of what you have read in this chapter may seem self- evident, try monitoring yourself every once in a while. Do you really make the most effective use of silences and pauses? Are you an interrupter? Do you actively listen?

32

Anyone, who takes into account their own weaknesses as well as those of others and consciously makes use of the above noted tools to steer a conversation, will have a decisive head start in almost all conversations!

PEOPLE COMMUNICATE MUCH LESS EFFECTIVELY AND CLEARLY THAN THEY THINK. JUST CONSIDER HOW OFTEN MISCOMMUNICATION IS GIVEN AS THE CAUSE OF A PROBLEM.

BY COMMUNICATING MORE CONSCIOUSLY, SUMMARISING AND REVIEWING YOUR PATTERNS REGULARLY, YOUR COMMUNICATION CAN BE GREATLY IMPROVED, HENCE: BETTER AGREEMENTS AND FEWER PROBLEMS.

ALWAYS MAINTAIN A GOOD POSTURE WHEN TELEPHONING. THAT MEANS: SITTING UP STRAIGHT, PEN AT THE READY AND WITH ALL OF THE RELEVANT DETAILS AT HAND!

You shouldn't run after money, but run across it
(Aristotle Onassis)

2. CREDIT MANAGEMENT

Credit management has, in the last few years, grown into an important part of company operations both at the domestic and international levels. Payment is, hopefully, the last phase in any transaction, and for the supplier, ultimately the most important step!

Good credit management not only provides a company with adequate cash flow; it improves liquid assets to an important extent and plays a crucial role in customer-account management.

The following example is meant to illustrate how credit management can affect bottom line results for any company. Here we have selected a company that, on average sells 12 shipments of $1million each, every month. Their open account terms are net 30(days).

For the purposes of this discussion, interest that could be earned on an investment on the open money market is 4%. The cost of borrowing on the open market is 10%.

a) **Every month that the product is in the hands of the customer and remains unpaid costs this company $40,000 in forgone interest income.**
b) **Typically, the company sells overseas and does not get paid for 90 days, on average. On every batch of shipments (12 × $1 million), they lose an average of $120,000 in lost interest income.**
c) **The company needs working capital and actually has to borrow $1 million on the open market at 10% for the year. Leaving aside closing costs, legal fees and the like, the cost of this capital totals $100,000 for the year.**

So far, the company, which could probably use the capital internally and make a profit greater than the 4% on the open market, has still lost approximately $1.5 million if we count 12 production runs for the year and the cost of bridge loan.

Note, so far, no payment is made later than 90 days and no collection or legal action has occurred. This company has total sales of $144 million a year. If they are lucky, and do not run into problems other than slow payments, over 1% of their total sales is eaten by capital that is in their customer's hands.

If the profit margin for this company is 5 percent, the dangers are becoming apparent. If they could get their payments within 60 days they would save roughly half a million dollars a year and might not need a bridge loan.

Again, this example does not provide for time, energy, company resources expended to collect the funds but leaves the opportunity cost of lost or floating capital at its most basic.

The following chart provides some indication of payment trends in Europe for 1997. It is possible to see how millions of dollars are lost every day by European businesses that do not receive payments on time.

Countries	Days Granted	Days Overdue	Total Days
Norway	21	6	27
Finland	19	10	29
Sweden	25	7	32
Denmark	27	7	34
Germany	23	11	34
Austria	29	8	37
Netherlands	27	19	46
United Kingdom	31	18	49
Ireland	35	16	51
France	48	10	58
Belgium	41	20	61
Spain	68	6	74
Italy	65	22	87
Portugal	50	41	91
Greece	75	19	94

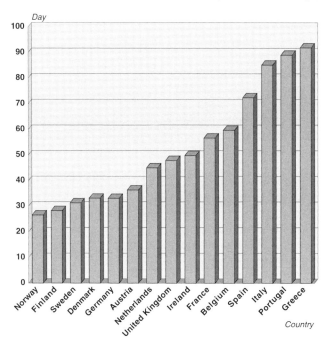

In the Netherlands, for instance, as in all of these countries, a considerable loss-creating item also exists: losses due to bankruptcy (approx. 3.7 billion guilders annually).

The total losses caused by bad or non-paying companies in the Netherlands amount to 8.3 billion guilders in the last year- roughly $4 billion US!

The above observations are applicable to *credit providing* companies (the suppliers). Not every one comes out a loser in this scenario; profit is made on the inability of these companies to have their outstanding debts paid on time. The banking industry, for instance, profits either way as thousands of companies are compelled to borrow money to bridge the many payment terms that have been exceeded in order to sustain viable working capital. On the other hand, banks lose potential billions from granting credit, because thousands of companies use their *suppliers* as banks.

Is it acceptable that YOU have to borrow expensive capital, so that your customer doesn't have to?

Prior to the import restrictions in Brazil (1997), Brazilian importers were using credit terms extended by foreign companies as working capital. This type of interest rate arbitrage which made the cost of using the foreign credit far cheaper than borrowing on the Brazilian market at rates of 35% per annum, can be found around the globe, especially in markets where the cost of borrowing is high.

The fact that it is becoming increasingly more "normal" for people and companies to delay payment of their bills is a curious yet not surprising phenomenon and businesses and consumers alike are encouraged to seek higher and higher credit limits. What seems to be forgotten in the equation is that payment is a concrete part of any agreement and that it will eventually have to be addressed.

The concept of 'I'll deliver X to you for price Y,' is, in reality, what most commercial transactions boil down to. Time is of the essence as far as delivery of goods is concerned but the reciprocal proposition does not hold true when it comes to payment. Strangely enough, it is

38

important that the supplier fulfil their agreements concerning quality, quantity and prompt delivery, but if the customer waits more than a month to pay, no one seems to bat an eyelid except, you, the credit manager who patiently waits.

The role of the credit manager in the organization

The task of the credit manager is to ensure that the payment terms of a contract are fulfilled. The manner in which this is effected is not only important for the cash flow within the company, but also affects many other bottom-line considerations.

The majority of companies make considerable investments in the marketing of their products and services. To attract new customers, representatives spare neither costs nor inconvenience; attractive reductions... Every means is utilized to draw a company into becoming a customer.

Once a business becomes a client, at the initial stages of the relationship, considerable effort is expended towards providing an optimum service, but in practice the special attention for such a customer quickly declines as time goes by. Supplier-customer contacts then run via the order department and the customer becomes "one of many".

In actual fact, few people really have extensive contact with the customer, except the credit and accounts receivable department. They send out the bills and will come into contact with the customer if and when problems arise. Oddly enough, when a bill is not paid, a strange coincidence may occur in the form of a complaint about the goods/services delivered, or that certain terms of the agreement have not been met.

At this point, it is up to the credit manager to solve the problem in the most expeditious manner while keeping the customer happy. The accounts receivable manager is therefore much more than an "accountant", he or she becomes the person who has contact with the customer at crucial and difficult moments that may affect future sales.

The credit manager occupies a very central role in the organization, and should be kept up-to-date concerning marketing and general corporate strategies of the company. The diagram below reproduces the central position of the credit manager:

Credit Manager in the organization

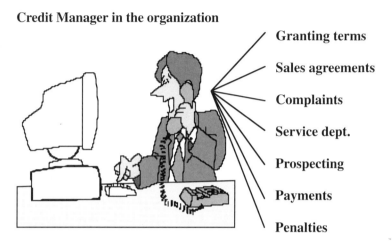

Granting terms

Sales agreements

Complaints

Service dept.

Prospecting

Payments

Penalties

- It is important that the debt collection or accounts receivable department be made aware of contractual amendments that have been agreed to with the customer.
- When contacting the customer, if it appears that they have complaints about the services or goods provided, the credit manager should respond accordingly and locate the source of these complaints within the company.
- Once the credit manager has contact with the customer, he or she can discuss their requirements and suggest alternate options for resolving any problems. The client can then be referred back to the Service or Sales departments if need be.
- The credit manager is often the first one to notice that the orders from certain customers are declining. In most cases this should indicate that there is a problem. Is the customer dissatisfied? Have they gone to a competitor? Are they having internal problems themselves? Conveying this information to the sales and customer service departments may help to salvage accounts and make you a valuable team player.

- The credit manager is obviously responsible for collecting payments. In this position, you may need to contact the account executive who is directly responsible for the sales and service of a particular account to get some matters resolved. Good internal communication is extremely important for a smooth transition to occur.
- If all other options have been exhausted, measures will have to be taken against a defaulting debtor. This can consist of blocking new deliveries, until the debt has been discharged. In almost all cases internal communication should precede these measures being taken.

The credit manager is an exceptionally important link in the company process. Their effectiveness depends just as much on their ability to communicate both internally and externally in a competent and pleasant manner.

Within a smaller company, credit should have contacts with most departments, from production and sales to service. Decisions must be taken in proper consultation so that a clear picture and policy can be presented to the customer.

The credit manager must think tactically and tactfully when dealing with and contacting the customer. Although it is his or her primary task to ensure that customers pay on time, this should be communicated in such a manner so that the customer comes away with a positive feeling about the transaction and the company.

This doesn't mean that you should let a customer walk all over you but being firm should not necessarily lead to the loss of an account.

A GREAT SALESPERSON CAN CLOSE A CUSTOMER IN A DAY, BUT A BAD CREDIT MANAGER CAN LOSE THAT CUSTOMER IN 5 MINUTES

A GOOD CREDIT MANAGER IS AT THE CENTER OF A COMPANY AND IS INFORMED ABOUT THE CORPORATION'S PRODUCTS AND SERVICES AND STRATEGY.

A credit manager is a financial marketer with a good sense of communication

3. COLLECTION

Col•lec•tion *n* 1 bank, make/undertake collections, undertake the collection of accounts, undertake debt collection(s), undertake to collect accounts.

Col•lect *v.t* 1 receive; 2 cash in.

The word "collection" has negative connotations for most people, caused by the historic and perhaps obvious associations with unscrupulous debt collection agencies, lawyers or even bailiffs. This association may have some validity, but in this book the concept of "collecting" outstanding amounts owed to your company is intended as the receipt of these amounts by you the credit manager!

Your Mission:
It should be the objective of every credit manager to collect as many debts as possible, within the shortest possible term, in as pleasant a manner as possible.

In this chapter we will examine what is necessary to achieve this goal. As the chapter progresses, it will become evident that proper organization and telephone technique will have a direct impact on your success.

Contracts
Payment by a debtor is based on a *contract*. At its most basic, the selling party is obliged to deliver the goods and services at a point and place in time while the buying party is obliged to deliver financial consideration in return for the delivered product.

As a result, it is important that a contract is made clear and reflects the intention of both parties from the outset. In practice that means agreements concerning the transaction must be made as unambiguous as possible so that delivery of and subsequent payment for the promised item can occur.

Why are contracts important to you?

In order for you to collect the amounts that are owed to you by a customer, you must have some idea of what is contained in your standard form contracts. Chances are your invoices do not include the full details of the agreement. While you need not become a corporate lawyer, having some idea and familiarity with the legal aspects of your company's type of transaction will be an asset to your career. If, for instance, you know that it is your company's policy never to amend a contract after the goods have been shipped, you will not be intimidated by a buyer who says he or she obtained a price concession when the goods were on the ship.

As discussed earlier, internal communication in your organization is vital to a successful business cycle. Your due diligence does not stop there. Any agreement that you have with a customer should have some basic elements. There are different rules around the world concerning contract law depending on the type of legal system in which you are located or are selling. Without going into all of the distinctions, some basic rules of common sense apply to just about any contract which will serve to make the credit manager's position as strong as possible:

1. The general terms and conditions should be clear and comprehensive.
2. The order/agreement should be in writing.
3. The invoice should be correct and filled out completely.
4. The invoice should be documented as much as is possible.

These practical tips help to keep vagueness, disputes and the chance of "lost" invoices to a minimum. Organization in advance of any shipment will pay dividends when it comes time for collection.

1. The general terms and conditions should be clear and comprehensive
Thousands of companies around the world still work without fixed or any general terms and conditions of sale. While these are essential for making clear your position as the supplier, in cases of disagreements or discussions, they also determine the rights and obligations of both parties. Moreover, failing to properly set out terms and conditions may result in having a set of fixed conditions imputed into your contract. Do you really want some foreign body determining your rights and obligations?

These are some issues that should be addressed in the general terms and conditions of your sales contracts. This list is not meant to be exhaustive but to give some guidelines for the formation of a valid sales contract applicable universally:

1. Offer and acceptance should be clear.
2. Amount owing specified
3. Is it a contract or a letter of intent
4. Identification of the parties and their [proper legal identity and capacity]
5. Definitions
6. Representations and Warranties
7. Date
8. Price
9. Currency
10. Description of goods
11. Scope of the contract- who and what is affected?
12. Payment terms
13. Methods of Payment
14. Payment obligations

15. Time
16. Delivery
17. Variations and adjustments (how and when)
18. Title and transfer of title
19. Risk
20. Insurance
21. Responsibility
22. Liability and Performance
23. Limitations of liability
24. Exclusions of liability
25. Penalties/damages
26. Force majeur
27. Hardship
28. Default and opportunity to cure default
29. Assignment
30. Tests and inspections and certifications
31. Representations and authority to represent
32. The contract constitutes the entire agreement
33. Confidentiality
34. Alternative dispute resolution
35. Choice of law
36. Litigation
37. Guarantees and Bonds
38. Jurisdiction
39. Venue
40. Notice
41. Waiver
42. Service

By approving the agreement, the buyer accepts the general terms and conditions from the seller. Should problems arise meanwhile, the supplier can therefore refer the customer to the conditions to which they themselves have agreed. The more you have set out in advance, the less you will need to interpret at a future date.

The customer should be *aware* of your delivery and payment conditions before the transaction is closed.

The terms and conditions should be clearly printed on all contracts.

Refer to them in your invoices! In this manner you can avoid nasty surprises if you unexpectedly find yourself in court with your customer. Key terms and conditions should be directly included on the invoice.

Frequently, a company's terms and conditions are crammed on to their invoice (front and back). Instead of relying on only the fine print a secondary document may be annexed or appended to the invoice and should be referred to explicitly on the front page of said invoice. This does not absolve you from getting a signed contract but allows for duplication of notice to your purchaser and avoids future ambiguity.

2. The order/agreement should be in writing
Written proof of the order or agreement can avoid a great deal of trouble. In both civil law and common law jurisdictions, the written contract is almost always upheld over the oral contract. GET IT IN WRITING!

This is especially important in the case of amended agreements (for example those deviating from the general terms and conditions), extra reductions, supplements etc….

Chapter 1 effectively demonstrated how easily miscommunication can occur between two people, imagine entire companies with multitudes of people. By setting up comprehensive written contracts such problems are quickly brought to the surface. In addition, both parties have written proof of their rights and obligations, which considerably reduces subsequent errors and disputes.

3. The invoice should be correct and filled out completely
Those spaces in the invoices that are to be filled are there for a reason and should not be left empty. It may seem obvious, but it is almost unbelievable how much still goes wrong in producing and sending out invoices. Of course the correct amount should be on the invoice, but also a clear description of what has been delivered. How it is addressed is also terribly important. By ensuring that the bill arrives directly to the proper party at the correct location avoids the "floating invoice". A great risk in large firms or organizations.

Some companies work with their own sale reference or purchase-order numbers; these should always be included on the invoice! Help yourself get paid faster, use their system if they have one.

It frequently occurs that supplements must be made due to various reasons. These should be kept as simple as possible; credit notes etc. add to the vagueness of the amount owing and result in slowing down the collection process. By deducting as much as possible on the invoice, with clear explanation, the process can be sped up considerably.

Invoice checklist
- Addressing; correct address, company, department, contact person
- Description of delivery; product/services, quantities, delivery location and date
- Clear specification of the amount, including possible supplements
- Reference or purchase order number of the other party
- Order date
- Person/department who did the ordering
- Clear statement of payment conditions
- Clear statement of the desired method of payment (bank account number!)
- Name and direct-dial number of the credit manager responsible

4. The invoice should be documented as much as is possible
Vendors require their invoices to be paid promptly and within the specified terms. Questions and uncertainties should be avoided. This can be achieved by providing the invoice along with copies of the most important documentation concerning the order.

Hardly anyone ever does that, despite the fact that it can be extremely practical. The customer does not even have to look at the quote or order confirmation, but can sign the invoice immediately.

Consider adding copies of the following documentation when invoicing:
- Order/order form
- Price Quotation
- Order confirmation
- Contract
- Signed delivery slip

It takes slightly more trouble to do this in practice, but can be of great use if quicker payment is your goal. No demands need to be sent, the credit manager does not have to be called and no subsequent interest losses are incurred!

The transaction cycle
Payment should not be addressed at the end of the transaction cycle but right at the very beginning. The entire process followed influences the speed of payment and is of paramount importance to the credit manager.

The transaction cycle

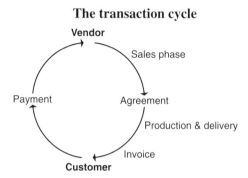

In the sales, production and delivery phase, maximum service and attention is directed towards the customer. In reality the attention given to a customer is greatest during the sales phase and, in most companies, will decline steadily during the cycle's progress. For our purposes in collections, a process located towards the end of the cycle, the longer the collection phase lasts, the less "friendly" the treatment of the customer becomes.

Evolution service- and collection-element

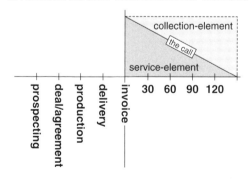

49

Unfortunately service appears to be inversely proportional to time in the business cycle. The longer the payment remains outstanding, the more the collection effort exists to the detriment of service. For the advancement of the supplier/customer relationship it is better to avoid the collection phase altogether, then customers will obtain optimum service and the cycle can continue unhindered. What can we do improve a difficult situation?

While collections appear to be an integral part of a credit manager's job description, this is a part that, with effective planning, can be minimized. The credit manager could contact the customer before invoicing for the first time. This first conversation has the character of providing a service, and consequently has a much greater positive effect and may allow you to find out any peculiarities about the buyer company's payment process.

Evolution service- and collection-element

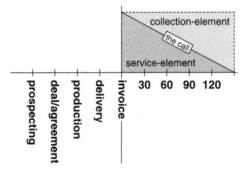

The credit manager could, for example, seek contact with the person responsible for the customer's accounts payable beforehand. That may seem unnatural or strange, but it is nevertheless very businesslike:

'Good morning Mr. Jones, you're speaking with Peter Farmer from Deliveries Ltd. Our company delivered 50 boxes of widgets yesterday, and I was just calling to check whether everything was in order?'
....
'Ah, perfect. So can I send the invoice today? I understand that you are responsible for the payment?'

50

....
'Then you can expect our invoice tomorrow. If you have any more questions, you can of course call me directly. Have you taken into account that our payment terms are 30 days?'
....
'Great. We look forward to receiving your payment and thank you once again for ordering your widgets from us."

In this sample conversation, the primary intention is to avoid problems with payment; the customer will perceive the contact as a service call. "An ounce of prevention is better than a pound of cure" is applicable to any collection situation.

The payment
Having discussed the importance of adequate preparation in the contractual and pre-payment parts of the business cycle, it is time to address the issue of payment and collecting on a particular outstanding debt.

Graydon recently surveyed 150 credit managers and asked them:

"How many days after an account is past due will you wait before calling a debtor?"

The responses were distributed as follows:
Within 10 days   04%
After 10-30 days   10%
After 31-60 days   29%
After 61-90 days   46%
After 91-120 days   07%
Never   04%

While we do wonder about the 4% that never call, roughly half of the credit managers surveyed indicated that they were willing to wait longer than two months before seeking contact with a debtor. This is of course quite understandable, because after all far fewer invoices remain outstanding after this amount of time, meaning that fewer telephone calls have to be made. Moreover, many members of the group perceived the task of making a collection call as a negative.

The longer an invoice has lapsed, the greater the chance that "something is wrong". A problem with the quality of goods and services, an incorrect invoice, a credit note that is still expected... There are numerous reasons why a payment might not have been made, or which can be used by the customer to delay payment.

By waiting for such an extended period of time, the credit managers were saving time initially by having to make less phone calls but were losing time and company resources in the long run. When problems surface only after a few months, it actually takes considerably more time to determine the problem and, if necessary, to straighten out the difficulties. The result was that payment was being delayed for even longer periods of time.

The demand phase
While the demand phase of any collection is indeed important in the drive to getting paid, it needs to be managed effectively. Almost every company has a series of standard form demand letters that become steadily more threatening and less friendly, the service element declining and the collection element increasing.

As is true with invoicing, the effectiveness of the reminder or demand letter depends strongly on its comprehensiveness and clarity. The time element also plays an additional role: from the moment when the reminder is sent, a clear signal is conveyed to the debtor concerning your company's position with respect to their delinquent payment. Using the demand letter effectively and correctly will assist not only in collecting the amount but in maintaining the relationship with the account.

Advantages of a written demand:
- Less expensive
- Can be completely automated
- Moment of issue can be determined accurately
- No problem regarding accessibility of contact person

Disadvantages of a written demand:
- Comes across as "standard"
- Relatively little effect
- Passive ➜ there is no interaction
- May not have been received

The most important disadvantage of a written reminder is that there is no direct contact; it is very easy to put the demand letter in the circular file (trash). The inherent danger in the "standard form principle" is that it becomes so standard that everyone waits for something else before reacting. Experience will show a debtor who always pays late exactly how many demands they can expect and how many they can ignore before things get serious and they actually have to remit.

It is therefore a **deadly** sin to put *"1st demand"* on the letter: this sends the message that there will be a 2nd, and perhaps even a 3rd demand. A persistent debtor will not pay any attention to such a payment reminder.

An overview of the various instruments available to the credit manager, and their various advantages and disadvantages follows below:

The greatest effect is achieved by visiting the customer, but that option can be discounted in practice due to the enormous amount of time involved. Nevertheless, in some cases such a visit must certainly be given consideration, for example with a very important customer who continuously fails to meet their obligations.

The best alternatives remaining are therefore written and telephone collection. The collection conversation, which will be discussed in extensive detail in the following chapter, is in practice an extension of a written payment reminder. After all, the debtor has already received one or two demands which have obviously not had the desired effect.

The written demand letter, much like the sales contract, the production and delivery of the goods and the invoicing, belongs among the actions completed prior to the telephone collection. The success of the collection conversation partially depends on the quality of the demand letter.

Written demands/payment reminder checklist

- Addressing; correct address, company(!), department, contact person
- Description of the delivered product/service, quantity, delivery location and date
- Clear specification of the amount owing, including possible adjustments
- Complete overview of **all** outstanding invoices
- Copy(ies) of invoice(s)
- Other party's reference or purchase order number
- Clear statement of the number of days by which terms have been exceeded
- Clear statement of the desired means of payment (bank account number!)
- Name and contact number of the credit manager responsible
- Request for **direct** contact if there is another reason for non-payment
- Interest provisions and penalties

A good demand letter will very much mirror what was set out in the original invoice. If the invoice was flawed, it will have a direct and negative impact of the effectiveness of the demand for payment.

The request for direct and immediate contact is very important; in this manner possible problems with the delivery or invoice come to the surface allowing for direct action to be taken. The credit manager's position may be improved at this point in time if he or she can indicate to the debtor that they had ample opportunity, prior to the letter and call, to point out the defects or problems with the goods purchased.

Penalties or sanctions
Sanctions are essential, but should be handled very carefully. It is probably not desirable to wield a club with the first demand but as time passes the need for stronger more draconian actions will become evident.

What sanctions are available to the credit manager? Various options will be discussed in chapter 5, but which can be summarized below as:

- Calculating interest & costs
- Cash on delivery only
- Blocking deliveries
- Recalling goods
- Hand over to debt collection agency
- Hand over to bailiffs
- Hand over to lawyer

Conclusion
By way of conclusion, the cycle that a transaction follows directly or indirectly influences eventual payment. With good internal organization, complete documentation and clear invoicing, many problems can either be avoided completely or minimized from the outset!

DO NOT GIVE A DEBTOR ANY OPPORTUNITY TO MAKE UP EXCUSES OR TO FIND SHORTCOMINGS IN ORDER TO AVOID PAYMENT!

GOOD CHANCES OF COLLECTION BEGIN WITH PROFICIENT AND CLEAR AGREEMENTS

AN INVOICE MAY BE YOUR CUSTOMER'S INVITATION FOR PAYMENT BUT IT SHOULD ALSO ACT AS A SIGNAL TO YOUR COMPANY TO START THE BALL ROLLING FOR COLLECTION ON THAT ACCOUNT.

Better to know the worst than to doubt
(J.L. de Haan)

4. PREPARING FOR THE COLLECTION CALL

The success of a collection conversation is, to a great extent, determined by the preparation made beforehand. It is not only important that the credit manager be aware of all the relevant information concerning the debtor and the outstanding debt(s), but determining the position of the company with respect to the debtor is also important. Preparing for the collection conversation consists of two phases:

1. Information phase
2. Positioning phase

The objective of the information phase is to enter into the conversation armed with as much information concerning the particular account as possible, so that unexpected problems, new developments or counter-arguments do not take you by surprise.

During the information phase, the credit manager makes themselves aware of the relevant data concerning the debt(s) and gets some background information on the debtor. The latter is unfortunately a detail that receives too little attention in practice. Namely that the fact a company pays a bill late or not at all, must not be viewed separately from the situation of the company itself. Imagine repeatedly calling a company that has gone into receivership or re-organization, you would be wasting valuable resources without knowing this fact and being able to provide an alternate payment plan or to register a claim in the appropriate legal jurisdiction.

The most important parts of the information phase are outlined below, followed by a brief explanation of the various points involved.

Information phase
1. Who is to be called? name, function, authority
2. Have all complaints been remedied?
3. Has all invoice information been prepared?
4. What is the total outstanding balance and what is that composed of?
5. What are the customer's past payment trends or practices?
6. How does this customer pay other suppliers?
7. What is the complaint history for this customer?
8. How many demands have been sent?
9. What is the credit limit?
10. What is their credit rating?

1. Who is to be called? → name, function, authority
Being able to question the correct contact person is vital to the efficiency of the conversation. Nonetheless, it is far more important that the credit manager be aware ahead of time of the responsibilities and authority of their conversation partner. This includes determining whether their conversation partner has the authority to make binding agreements on behalf of the purchaser. Who can and will eventually sign the money transfer?

If the credit manager doubts the authority of their contact person and the outstanding debts are coming to a crisis point, then they should look "higher up" the corporate food chain. Once this new contact is made, the employee can no longer use his/her boss as an excuse in the event that new payment difficulties arise.

58

2. Have all complaints been remedied?

A collection conversation should never slip into a discussion of breaches in the initial agreement or degenerate into mutual expression of dissatisfaction. Prior to the conversation, the mechanics of the order should have already been dealt with.

For that purpose, consider briefly the transaction cycle: payment flows as a result of the supplier having met all their commitments. If we approach the debtor with all their shortcomings in not meeting the agreed upon commitments in the transaction, we should first be convinced that we have fulfilled *our* part of the agreement.

Your psychological position, in this respect, will be buttressed. It is much easier to make a collection call knowing that your company has discharged its obligations. This will not happen in every circumstance but if a small matter needs to be resolved, it will serve to address it prior to making a call asking for payment.

3. Has all invoice information been prepared?

It seems a logical thing to say, but it cannot be emphasized enough: if a telephone collection conversation is to be made, the credit manager *must have all relevant documentation at hand!* Being ready is the key word in this instance. If you are referring to an invoice, don't be put in the position of having to go and look for it and having to call the other party back.

4. What is the total outstanding balance and what is it composed of?

Prior to the conversation, the credit manager must decide which part or parts of the payment they wish to address and have a backup plan ready to propose to a recalcitrant debtor. Are you asking for the payment in full, payment only for those goods shipped or future payments for goods to be shipped?

By understanding where your claim exists in the transaction cycle, you may gain some leverage. It may be that the buyer has only received half of the goods ordered and needs the rest. This knowledge will prove advantageous.

5. What are the customer's past payment trends or practices?

It is very useful to delve briefly into a customer's previous payment record. If it appears that the payment pattern has recently deteriorated, this may signal that the buyer is experiencing a particular crisis. You then need to determine whether your company has had any responsibility (i.e. product dis-satisfaction) for that crisis or whether the problem is driven by other factors, for example liquidity problems or market problems. Determining the source of the crisis, if indeed it exists, will allow you to tailor your conversation with the debtor.

6. How does this customer pay other suppliers?

The payment patterns of a customer to third parties reveals a great deal about the buyer's ability to pay. Tying in with point number five, if you notice an across the board slow-down in payment, there is a strong likelihood that the slowdown has nothing to do with your product. It is unlikely that all suppliers are not providing adequate service. Going into the conversation, you will know that some other factor is affecting payment. Is it internal or external?

The big question is of course how that information can be acquired! This can be done in two ways: the first option is to request a trade evaluation report on a company, the second option is make your own inquiries.

Company trade evaluation reports can be requested from credit reporting companies like Graydon when ordering a credit report. These will contain important information concerning a company's payment performance, as well as data relating to the financial situation, the structure of the company, the management and the credit limit.

For those who want to acquire the information on their own, you only need know the names of a few other suppliers to the customer. Consequently, a colleague in the company concerned can be called provided this is an allowable practice in your particular jurisdiction.

7. What is the complaint history for this customer?

The complaint history says something about overall customer satisfaction and their readiness to co-operate in finding solutions. If the customer concerned is a chronic complainer who complains about the smallest or most insignificant details, you can still use this information as an argument: "You always attach value to strict observance of the contract; so do we!"

Customers who never complain are (probably) satisfied. Remind the customer that you have fulfilled all agreements in the past and that it is now their turn!

8. How many demands have been sent?
A slow paying debtor will have probably received several written demands. Before reaching for the telephone, the credit manager should know how many demands have already been sent and thus, how many the debtor has put aside!

9. What is the credit limit?
Many companies operate an internal credit limit. This is an excellent instrument for keeping credit risks under control. A check of the current outstanding balance with regard to the credit limit should form part of the preparations for the conversation. On the one hand, to estimate the risk involved, and on the other, because a reduction of the credit limit could eventually be used as a sanction.

10. What is the buyer's credit rating?
The credit rating of any customer can be of vital importance. After all, the debtor has *your* money for constructive purposes in their possession! The credit manager should consider whether something is already known about the customer's liquidity problems internally within the organization (with Sales for example). Requesting credit information can, of course, be very helpful in this case.

Many credit analysts make the mistake of relying on old information. A company's balance sheet changes year to year and quarter to quarter, getting the best up-to-date information will allow you greater insight into a company's financial position and alert you to negative trends.

> *He who knows where to find what he does not know,*
> *knows enough*

The positioning phase

Once the above information has been gathered, the credit manager is aware of several facts which boil down to who they are calling, which payment exactly they wish to address and what are the general circumstances surrounding the transaction and the buyer company.

This knowledge is nonetheless still not complete nor satisfactory. They must also understand the *objective* of the call. What is their own company's position compared to that of the debtors? What is the commercial importance of this transaction, this relationship? Is it more important to get the money, or is it more important to keep the customer as a customer? Determining that relationship is known as "positioning".

During the positioning phase, the following questions should be addressed:

• Why are we calling?
• What is the objective?
  → an outstanding unpaid account
  → an unacceptable pattern or payment behavior
• What is our choice of strategy?
• Where do we want to go with this customer?
  → in the short term
  → in the distant future

These questions offer a thought process to the credit executive prior to making a call. The resulting effect will boil down to two options:

1. The debtor pays and remains a customer
3. The debtor pays and is no longer a customer

It appears evident that the first option is preferable by far to the second. Everything ultimately revolves around keeping the transaction or business cycle in continuos motion. This is to the advantage of both the supplier and the customer!

Nevertheless, it is sometimes unavoidable that we no longer *want* a certain company as a customer, or that we want a company to remain a customer, but only under the condition that they change their payment practices.

In too many cases that decision is either delayed far too long or not taken at all. Companies attach too much value to the "sales turnover" a customer provides, despite the fact that no money is actually coming in. Still, by performing calculations more often, we would discover that we would rather lose some customers than be "rich" in non-paying clients. Again, this very much depends on your company's objective of which you must be unambiguously aware. If the entire sales exercise is aimed at market penetration and market share, payment may take a back seat to capturing a particular market segment for the long term.

If we consider that a company meets their outstanding payment obligations and remains a satisfied customer, we have in principle achieved the ideal. We call this situation:

WIN – WIN

If, at the end of the day, we receive the amounts that are owed even if it has the consequence of losing the customer, then we have another viewpoint:

WIN – LOSE

Before coming to a decision about the strategy to be followed, internal consultation is necessary especially in the case of a win – lose situation. In collaboration with the sales manager responsible, the credit manager must consider to what extent a win -win or win -lose situation is acceptable.

Within every organization responsibility is distributed in different ways: whereas in one company the credit manager has the authority to decide a win -lose situation independently, in another organization that will be the responsibility of the sales or marketing manager.

The most ideal situation is however when both the credit manager and the sales manager arrive at a decision in collaboration. Everyone has different input, but everyone is ultimately working towards the same goal: an optimum result for their own company!

Conclusion
Superior results will be achieved thorough preparation as opposed to making calls willy-nilly as accounts come due. It takes slightly more time to collect all the necessary information and to study it, but you will be well prepared and be able to address all of the issues during your first conversation. You will not have to call back again or make decisions during the conversation that you might later regret because you were uninformed at the time.

IF YOU KNOW HOW YOUR CUSTOMERS PAY OTHERS, YOU WILL KNOW HOW MUCH CAN BE RECOVERED.

SEVENTY FIVE PERCENT OF YOUR CHANCES FOR SUCCESSFUL COLLECTION IS DETERMINED BY YOUR INTERNAL ORGANISATION.

ALWAYS ENSURE THAT YOU ARE BETTER PREPARED THAN THE OTHER PARTY. THE FACT THAT YOU ARE CALLING HAS PROVIDED YOU THE ADVANTAGE OF HAVING TAKEN THE FIRST STEP; AS A RESULT OF YOUR PREPARATION YOU MAINTAIN THE ADVANTAGE.

KNOWLEDGE IS POWER!

You can't make an omelet without breaking eggs
(French expression)

5.   The Collection Call

In this chapter, we will examine all aspects of the actual collection conversation. A collection conversation does not by definition have to be unpleasant or unfriendly; on the contrary, the aim is to continue the customer service process while insuring payment on a delinquent account! If we remain conscious of the mutual importance of the supplier and the customer, a continuation of the working relationship is possible.

Initial contact with the debtor usually begins at its most basic in the form of a contact with the debtor organization's telephone operator/receptionist. This initial contact can be used to your advantage.

The operator/receptionist
The operator/receptionist is an entity within each organization that should not be underestimated. Take advantage of your conversation with the receptionist to mine as much information as possible about the person you need to contact. While some receptionists have absolutely no clue or are only aware of the people on paper, others have been around for a long time and are a wealth of information if you can get them to talk.

The receptionist has some awareness of everyone's position, job description and responsibilities within the corporation. They may also have knowledge of schedules, sick days and return dates for specific individuals. In addition, because they take all of the company's calls, they will not be scripted in advance to avoid your particular call unless it is a very small company and even then, in the day to day volume of calls they may forget.

If you are calling a certain contact for the first time, the operator has to connect you through to the right person. It is a waste not to maximize your opportunity to mine information at that time; the operator can provide some background concerning your contact:

"Debtor Ltd., good morning!"

"Good morning, you're speaking with Jack Smith from Suppliers Ltd. Can you tell me who is responsible in your company for accounts payable?"

"Of course, that would be Mr. Williams."

"Ah. What is his initial?"

"It's P for Peter."

"Thanks very much. Could you connect me through to him please?"

"Of course, one moment....."

By means of that short conversation, you are already much wiser; not only have you achieved being connected to the right person, but you now know their full name and something about their authority and position in the company!

The following sentences are therefore to be strongly discouraged:

"Could you connect me to someone from the credit department?"

"I'm looking for someone from accounting."

"I would like to speak to someone in financial administration."

By using these openers, you do not have a name, you do not have a position and you have to play the guessing and avoidance game with someone who may be more skilled and prepared than the receptionist. Avoid words such as "accounting, financial administration or creditor administration."

Accounting and financial administration are too vague and the chance of finding yourself with the wrong person is great. Creditor administration is basically correct, yet reveals nothing about the authority of the person who will be on the end of the line. Moreover, that term will not be in use in every company, meaning we are obliged to give extra information.

"The accounts payable manager" or "the person who makes payments" leaves nothing unclear and gives a greater guarantee that we will be talking to someone who is in the position to make a decision and/or a commitment.

Absence of the right person

As is often the case, person we need is on sick leave or on holiday (which may be one reason why the payment is late in the first place), it is often worthwhile checking the length of their absence with the receptionist. After all, the absent employee's colleagues have other interests; it is probably easier for them to put all the *"moaning"* on hold for as long as possible......

If you get the feeling that you are being given the brush off, the operator/receptionist is the right person to have these suspicions confirmed or denied!

Sickness or absence in general can be an awkward obstacle for the credit manager. What is the best course of action in such a case?

- Ask for a colleague with the same function;
- If they are not available; ask for a subordinate
- If they are not available or cannot respond; ask for the absent person's manager

It will occur fairly regularly that a colleague will have you believe that there is no one with the authority to make the payment.

THAT IS NOT TRUE!

Business did not grind to a standstill because Joe Smith in accounts payable took his family to Disneyland. There are always other people with authority in a company. The president, for example, *always* has full authority. That does not in any way mean that the C.E.O. should be directly approached in these cases, but it can sometimes be a very real option. For example, if you have repeatedly tried to get the right person on the line for a long period of time.

Often times if you do get the president of a mid-sized company on the line, you may see very rapid results. They will be angry that the matter got to them and will take internal action to remedy the situation.

The collection conversation: introduction
Assuming that we have now been connected, and that we have got the desired person on the telephone, begin the collection conversation with three important elements:

• Check contact person
• Self introduction
• State objective

Check whether you have been connected with the right person. Our conversation partner will have given his/her name when they picked up the telephone, but check what it is that they do. Maybe they changed jobs; maybe they aren't the right party:

"Mr. Williams, I understand that you are responsible for accounts payable?"

This question forces a confirmation or denial. It also means that we express recognition of the "importance" and position of the conversation partner. Furthermore, it indicates that we "have done our homework"; we have taken the trouble to inform ourselves about their position within the company. Not only is this friendly, but it indicates that they are dealing with a professional and resolute person and will block them from claiming that someone else is responsible later on in the conversation.

70

By saying his/her name it confirms that we have made a mental note of it signaling interest

The self-introduction consists of giving your own name, first name and surname, and the *full* company name, including the legal form (Ltd., PLC, or partnership firm).

"Good morning, you're speaking with Peter Smith from Friendly Suppliers Incorporated."

These two parts can be reversed. It is better with companies where you are anticipating difficulty to get an admission from the responsible party that they are in charge, prior to giving them your company name. If they are expecting your call, they may deny responsibility if they think that they can get away with it.

Now that both parties know with whom they are dealing, it is time to reveal the objective of the conversation.

"I'm calling concerning invoice xxx, which should have been paid 2 months ago at the latest. Can you tell me why it hasn't been paid?"

A short and concise account of the problem: the invoice, and when this should have been paid. Consequently, this type of ***OPEN-ENDED question should always be used!***

By asking "why" the conversation partner is put on the spot in a friendly manner. They must now explain why the company has not fulfilled their part of the bargain. It is often not so difficult to acknowledge something, but to have to say why is often a lot more awkward…

The collection conversation: information phase
Following the introduction and the presentation of the objective of the conversation, there should be a response from the conversation partner. They will now provide information about the reasons for which the invoice in question has not been paid. From this point on there are many possibilities, excuses (valid or invalid), complaints about services/products or even a blunt refusal to pay.

Regardless of the reason that is given, there is one golden rule: the reason for non-payment should be overcome or cleared out of the way from the outset. The first action to be taken consists of *isolating* the problem. This means that the credit manager checks that the reason given is the *only* cause of the outstanding payment delay. The way in which to do this is to sum up the problem and bounce it back:

"So the invoice hasn't yet been paid because you haven't had the time?"

"How unfortunate that you've been ill. Is that the only reason for the bill still being outstanding?"

Register exactly what the customer tells you: this gives you the opportunity to return to this later (interest) and to check whether a certain customer is consistent!

By isolating the problem, you exclude the possibility that other excuses or reasons suddenly come to the surface. A short summary re-formulated and in a questioning form, bounced back to the conversation partner, provides the basis for a mutual **solution**.

The solution will not be as easy in every case. The problem can be beyond the powers of the accounts payable or accounting department, and in some cases, the problem will be with the company *itself*.

72

It is important in all cases to consider and have ready possible solutions. This means: mutual consideration, coming up with ideas, looking into the various options and probably furnishing some information yourself.

It is not always an easy task to arrive at a solution acceptable to both parties. Both parties frequently have other priorities, options and problems, so a mutually acceptable agreement must be keenly negotiated. As negotiation is an enormously important part of the collection conversation, a complete chapter of this book has been dedicated to it, chapter 7.

The collection conversation: the agreement
So you've isolated the problem that has lead to the delay, you have presented a possible solution, now an **agreement** can be made. An agreement that must lead to the invoice being paid. The agreement must be unequivocal. In order to arrive at a firm commitment, the agreement should contain the following elements:

• Who takes what action?
• When exactly: dates!
• The exact amount that is going to be paid
• The exact date on which payment will be paid
• The method of payment

The last element, the method of payment, is exceptionally relevant because it can regularly lead to communication breakdown. One company works with tele-banking, the other with a file once a month to the bank and another fills in and sends off credit transfer forms.

It is clear that each method of payment takes a certain amount of time. In the case of credit transfers to a bank, a sum can "float around" for several days. If both parties properly inform one another about the method of payment, a realistic date can be agreed upon at which time the amount should be transferred to the supplier, avoiding any misunderstandings. This is especially important with foreign accounts when you are dealing with cross-border transfers and different banking systems.

The collection conversation: the summary
"Clarity": is the key word, what it's all about. The credit manager has still not concluded the agreement until it has been summarized and presented to the conversation partner for approval.

"Agreed, Mr. Williams. Once more so that we are all on the same page: I'll now fax you a copy of the invoice directly, and then you will ensure that it is processed immediately and sent to the bank tomorrow with all the other payments. In the unlikely event of there being any problem with the invoice, you'll contact me today. With everything as agreed, we'll have the money within four working days!"

Note, you have used the following key words: *now, directly, immediately, today* and have set definitive time limits.

If the other party agrees with that summary, you have a solid agreement! You now know exactly what you can expect. Should it later transpire that the agreement *hasn't* been fulfilled, the matter can be addressed very concretely with the other party...

If you are extremely worried about the situation and can get the other side to co-operate, write a brief summary of your conversation and asked them to initial it for your file. This may be unacceptable to the other side but if you can get this type of acknowledgement, it will reinforce their obligations and give you a written record of your agreement.

The collection conversation: the conclusion
Of course we are not assuming that the contract will be disregarded. The trick is to show the customer your appreciation for their co-operation, and the **expectation** that they will ensure that everything goes according to what has been agreed.

Expressing expectation is a signal of trust, ultimately the basis of every collaboration!

74

"Well, Mr. Williams, I'm pleased that we've rapidly reached a solution together. I also hope that this means everything has been arranged satisfactorily."

The elements of a collection conversation are listed below in summary form:

1. The operator/receptionist
- Ask about responsibility
- Gain information about the contact person

2. Introduction
- Check contact person
- Give own name and complete company name
- State objective

3. Information phase
- Exchange of information
- Isolate problem
- Consider and offer solutions
- Define solution

4. Agreement
- Acceptable for both parties
- Who takes what action?
- When exactly: dates!
- The exact amount that is going to be paid
- The exact date on which payment will be made
- The manner of payment

5. Summary
- Short summary of the agreement made
- Approval from the other party

6. Conclusion
- Express appreciation
- Express expectation

Conclusion

In a logical and clearly structured collection conversation you will come across as professional and the course of the conversation with the contact will run in a pleasant and natural manner. Agreements should be 100% clear, always *summarize* what has been said and have it confirmed by the customer.

It is important to speak with the right person. This originates with the operator/receptionist; be as informed as possible about the full name, function, position, responsibility and authority of your contact person.

Isolating the problem not only defines the conversational issues, but also avoids you discovering afterwards that that there were other problems or reasons blocking payment. If you isolate and state the problem, you will be aware of the exact conditions that must be met in order to receive payment as arranged.

Agreements must be made as clear and concrete as possible so that you come away knowing that not only *this* payment will be made, but also *how, what, how much, when* and *where!*

AN UNATTAINABLE OR UNREALISTIC AGREEMENT IS WORSE THAN NO AGREEMENT AT ALL.

PROBLEMS ARE THERE TO BE SOLVED.

A PROBLEM IS NOT A DISASTER: AT LEAST YOU KNOW THE REASON FOR YOUR CUSTOMER'S FAILURE TO PAY!

REGISTER EXACTLY WHAT THE CUSTOMER TELLS YOU: THIS GIVES YOU THE OPPORTUNITY TO RETURN TO THE STATEMENT AT A LATER POINT AND TO CHECK WHETHER A SPECIFIC CUSTOMER'S BEHAVIOUR IS CONSISTENT!

He who knows nothing, must believe in everything
(M. von Ebner-Eschenbach)

6. Counter-arguments

Counter-arguments, our way of politely putting the term excuse, are frequent and ever-present in the collection field. Debtors can be enormously creative in making up excuses, reasons and stories why a payment has not been made. Many of these "counter-arguments" are legitimate, many others are not.

In this chapter, we will devote our effort to techniques for dealing with counter-arguments. In addition, the most often used counter-arguments will be discussed, as will methods to determine the level of truth and the best ways to respond to the various counter-arguments.

All possible counter-arguments can be broken down into three main categories:

1. Do want to, but was prevented
2. Don't want to
3. Do want to, but can't

One piece of knowledge should always be in the back of the credit manager's mind:

No one likes to pay!

There are so many reasons why this truism applies to our collection problems. These range from basic psychology of having got what you want and not wanting to pay for it at a later point in time, to purely financial considerations where it is to the customer's advantage to delay payment as long as possible in order to profit from the interest on the funds not disbursed. Regardless of the reasons, you need to get paid.

Counter-arguments: the technique
Most people respond to a counter-argument with a "counter-argument". We hear an argument, and begin immediately with our own opposing argument:

"I'm sorry, but I have not had any time to do it!"
"No time? Do you mean to tell me that in 2 months you haven't had a spare five minutes?!?"

This very human and often logical response is not **correct manner for dealing with a counter-argument, however tempting.**

Someone who delivers an argument is *expecting* the other party to counteract it with another argument. In actual fact, that person is bracing themselves for the counter-attack and is armed with fresh arguments or counter-arguments.

Whoever wants to come out of a discussion on top must show understanding and respect for their conversation partner. In practice that means: **take a position that *isn't* directly opposed to the other.** Put another way: go along with their arguments, show understanding and put yourself in their shoes.

"Hey, where were you? Didn't we agree that you'd come and help me move? Everything went wrong because you weren't there! I'm pretty annoyed with you!"

"Yeah, I can imagine you're upset. I'd have also felt the same way if I'd been you! I feel really bad that I put you in a difficult spot because our arrangement didn't pan out!"

"Oh. Well, I'm glad that you realize that yourself."

"Of course, there's no other way of seeing it..."

This shows how, by "going along with" the other party, the pointed edge of their argument can be blunted. It is very easy to remain angry with someone who continuously resists and defends themselves, but if someone goes along with them then the pressure is quickly dissipated.

That means that the other party is now once more open to other explanations; by such means an awkward discussion is avoided and the conversation is opened up.

This conversation technique comes down to "endorsing" the explanations and counter-arguments of the other party, an exceptionally useful technique. Endorsing can for example be:

"Yes, I understand.................,
"I can imagine................,
"It's a logical response................,
"Well, I'd have reacted in the same way................,
"You're absolutely right on that point................,
"That is indeed most annoying................,

BUT................!

Endorsing does not mean agreement with the customer or with their particular version of the facts. On the contrary: it is a conversation technique designed to move away from negative confrontation into positive resolution.

Counter-arguments: check for authenticity
A counter-argument can be legitimate; an excuse is not necessarily a story! In a certain sense, every counter-argument is 100% real because we are being confronted with it and action must be taken.

To be able to respond to a counter-argument in the effective manner, it is important to be able to check it for authenticity. This does not translate into accepting the explanation, but allowing for **questioning** into the background.

Each explanation should be taken at face value. Ultimately, we are not only calling to solve the problem *now*, but also to ensure that it does not happen in the future.

The position of your company with regard to the customer determines to a great extent the manner in which questioning is continued. During the positioning phase, the point of departure has already been determined: a win – win situation or a win – lose situation. The questioning takes place in accordance with the decided upon position:

- friendly
- forceful
- confronting

A telephone collection conversation has the objective of getting money. The counter-arguments provide reasons why something has happened or what will occur. At the moment of confrontation, the objective is to obtain **information** whether it leads to immediate resolution or eventual payment.

This information is necessary to estimate the seriousness of the situation, to be able to learn something from it, to obtain an expectation of resolve and to be able to arrive at a firm agreement. The following matters concerning the problem must be brought to light:

- Cause
- Consequence
- Duration
- Seriousness
- Action that should be taken by the debtor
- Action that we can undertake ourselves

A counter-argument always consists of a **problem**: the invoice has not been received, is lost, and is floating around within the organization. The goods/services were poor, agreements have not been fulfilled, there aren't the financial resources, the accountant is sick...

A problem always requires a **solution**. The correct manner to respond to a counter-argument is to strive for an eventual solution. In 90% of collection cases, the problem is with the debtor, so it is only logical to have them consider the solution as well.

"It's irritating that Mr. Williams has been ill, and for two weeks! If you speak to him give him my regards for a speedy recovery!" (Endorsing)

"In the meantime, what can we think up to solve this problem? Isn't there anyone else for example who can sign the invoice?" (Possible solution)

If we want to check the validity of an answer, the best check is in the solution. It is not so difficult to make up a problem, but to make up a solution has never been easy.

People *always* respond to a problem by seeking a solution. Problems without solutions are scarce! That means that we can expect a company to be in the position to solve their own problems; if it seems that this is not the case, then often something strange is afoot, which could indicate the explanation given is false or untrue.

This technique is often deployed automatically:

"It's ten thirty! Why are you so late? Where have you been!" (Problem)

"It was really busy at the office, I worked late." (Counter-argument, story)

"Why didn't you just give me a quick call then?" (Check through solution)

The nice thing about this method is that it is very positive. The other party is taken at their word, and in the meantime we are on the way to *our* objective: the solution to our problem!

82

No one does anything without it benefiting them. Put differently: people are always looking for an *advantage*, something that they want, that will make them better off. The moment you succeed in convincing the other party that it is to their advantage to do something, you have reached your objective.

"It would nevertheless be good for Mr. Williams if a solution is reached while he is out sick, otherwise he'll have mountains of work to deal with when he gets back!" (Advantage).

In this scenario, you are offering to help Mr. Williams as well as the person on the other end and putting up a potential solution to the problem at hand. Moreover, if the person says no to your offer, they are not only denying you but are causing more problems for the illusive Mr. Williams, problems that may come back to haunt them when Mr. Willliams returns to an office buried with paper.

Counter-arguments: the solution
In sum, there are a number of steps that can be taken to counteract "explanations" in the correct manner:

1. Endorsing
   - Interest
   - Sympathy

2. Continuing questioning
   - problem
   - cause
   - consequence
   - duration
   - seriousness

3. Check authenticity
   - Solution?
   - Action taken by the debtor
   - Action that we can undertake ourselves

4. Solution
   - Advantage for the debtor

Counter-arguments: an overview

There are many imaginable counter-arguments, and for every one of these so-called explanations numerous responses are possible. We have provided a short list of the most frequent counter-arguments, including a number of good possible responses. The following counter-arguments will be discussed:

1. In a meeting.
2. Sick.
3. You are calling at a most inopportune moment.
4. I am just the temporary replacement.
5. The accounting is contracted out.
6. Invoice has not yet been approved.
7. Invoice never received.
8. The payment is on the way.
9. Payment went wrong.
10. Something not in order with product/services/invoice.
11. We have different payment arrangements.
12. Have not had time.
13. Forgotten.
14. We have no money!

As previously stated, there are three categories of counter-arguments:

1. Want to, but was prevented.
2. Don't want to.
3. Want to, but can't.

These categories are modified by the following problems:
1. Accessibility
2. Unwillingness
3. Dispute/complaint
4. Indifference
5. Impotence/liquidity problems

If we look at the list of fourteen counter-arguments provided above, we see that numbers 1 through 6 are problems of "accessibility", numbers 7 to 9 may fall within the category of "unwillingness", number 10 in the category of "Dispute/complaint", numbers 11 to 13 are "indifference" and finally number 14 falls under "Impotence/liquidity problems".

Accessibility
Accessibility is an awkward problem, which usually translates into delay. When the right person is absent, no agreements can be made and a solution is no closer to being found. The golden rule in **all** cases concerning accessibility is never to let the initiative slip out of our hands. That means: we call back at an **agreed upon** time!

1. In a meeting
An explanation or excuse that is frequently used. Meetings are an unavoidable and integral part of the modern business life. We cannot change that, but we should try to arrange an alternative or to obtain clarification:

Your conversation could go something like this when faced with *"the meeting"*:

a) "Yes of course. When does the meeting finish? Great, then I'll call back at..."

b) "No worries. When does the meeting finish? Could you make sure to tell him that I'll call back at ... and that it concerns an outstanding bill?"

c) "Yes, they're unavoidable. Is there someone else who works in accounts payable?"

d) "Is this a regular permanent meeting day? When is a good time to call?"

2. Sickness
Sickness is and remains an awkward subject, and not only for the person in question. The great disadvantage of sickness is that it is hardly ever possible to estimate exactly how long it will last. In these cases always look for an alternate responsible party. As soon as the contact person is better and can be contacted you can again call back and show interest in their sickness. Remember, people love to talk about themselves, illness is rarely an exception.

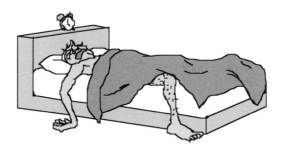

a) "How unpleasant! Nothing serious I hope? Is there someone who is filling in for them?

b) "Oh dear, that happens. Do you know with what? I'll call back next Monday, and see whether she's better or not."

c) "How unpleasant. For you as well, you must be extra busy! So, shall we try and sort out the reason for my call as quickly as possible?"

d) "I'm sorry to hear that. Could you please make sure to give him the message when he gets back that I called about an outstanding invoice, number xx? I'll call back again next Monday."

3. You are calling at a most inopportune moment
Another counter-argument that occurs frequently. If you truly think about it, it's never a great time for a debtor to discuss amounts that they owe you. They could have dealt with the issue at any number of "opportune" moments prior to your call. This is a counter-argument that can be easily checked for validity.

a) "That's annoying, because I will have to disturb her a second time anyway. It concerns an outstanding bill; if we could take a quick look at it together, we'd both be free of the problem."

b) "Excuse me. When would it be more convenient?"

c) "Indeed that's always annoying, but I don't need much time."

d) "You're quite right, because I'm calling about an outstanding bill(!)"

e) "Of course that's possible. If you could write down this invoice number and take a look for it later, then I'll call back in the afternoon".

f) "Oh dear! Is there perhaps somebody else with whom I can speak concerning the outstanding invoice?"

g) "Most annoying, but it's also highly inconvenient for us that the invoice still hasn't been paid!"

In fact, there are three options: first of all try to get some attention regardless of the inconvenience (check authenticity), secondly, try to get a colleague on the line, and as a last option make a new appointment.

"Inopportune" concerns priorities; the person is apparently busy with something, which they consider to be more important than your telephone call. Your money is not a priority to them.

4. I am just the temporary replacement
A replacement who cannot or may not do the work involved is no replacement. Someone else is in charge, find out who it is.

a) "Thanks, I am really glad that I could come to you with my question!"

b) "That's well arranged! It concerns the following......"

In the first instance we assume that the replacement can help us. If they consequently indicate that they are "only" the replacement:

c) "Sorry? I thought you said that you were the *replacement*......"

d) "Oh, but listen it's nothing complicated. It's about an invoice that hasn't been paid, I have all the details here..."

A temporary replacement never knows exactly what's going on, or what sort of agreement has been made. In these cases try to guide the conversation and the result:

e) "Mr. Williams always transfers the amount over directly. Could you also do that please?"

f) "Ms. Jones is always on top of her accounts payable, we've never had a problem before, it Would be a shame to start while she is away".

5. The accounting is out-sourced:
In these cases it is important to ascertain what exactly has been contracted out, is that the administration, or is it the actual transfer of funds?

With this counter-argument there is a danger that we will not be able to keep the initiative in our own hands. Contacting the accountants *ourselves* is an option that needs to be explored; get the details.

Point out to the debtor that the responsibility is and ultimately remains theirs to pay the bill, whether it is contacted out or not! The accounting firm did not sign the original contract!

a) "That's handy, that'll save you a pile of work. Can you give me a reference number so that I can call them for the check! It concerns the following..."

b) "I can imagine, but how are we going to arrange for the invoice to be paid?"

c) "I understand. Would it be a solution if I give your accountant a call?"

d) "That's a great service! When is your accountant going to set up the payment?"

6. Invoice has not yet been approved

This problem can fall both into the category "accessibility" and the category "dispute/complaint". In the first case, it has not yet passed through the "administrative process", in the second case there is something wrong with the delivery, or with the invoice.

In each case persistent questioning is required in order to ensure that the correct information comes to the surface.

a) "How awkward. Could you tell me who is handling this task? Can I contact him/her to discuss matters?"

b) "Invoices can make long trips can't they? But this one's been away for a long time! Who can I contact to help ease this delay?"

c) "Oh, how annoying. Is there something the matter with the invoice? Do you have any idea what the reason is? If I call back tomorrow at…could you clear up the matter for me?

d) "That's not so good. Is there perhaps some ambiguity that I can clear up?"

e) "Ah. Could you please connect me to the person that has to authorize it?"

f) "I know that an invoice has to pass through a few people with us, same for you?"

g) "Oh dear, I hope that there isn't a problem. It would be pity if that should only come to the surface now!"

7. Invoice never received

The routes taken by invoices are sometimes unfathomable. All the more surprising that more mail isn't lost! Strangely enough, it is nearly always bills or checks that can't seem to get delivered...

In the case of the mysteriously missing invoice, you have several options. One is to take the person at their word and re-issue and invoice. Try to do it instantly by fax, while they are on the line.

Usually the excuse of the missing invoice falls within the category "unwillingness". You might ask whether the debtor has received the three reminder notices that have also been sent or whether they have also disappeared. Never let on that you do not believe them, but do be critical.

a) "That's strange, we haven't had it returned by the Post Office. Your address is... isn't it?"

b) "Oh? And you haven't had our follow-up notices either? Why haven't you responded to them?"

c) "That makes payment difficult, doesn't it? It's a good thing that I called... You know what? I'll fax you a copy of the invoice, and you can ensure that it is paid today?"

d) "That's strange. I'll fax you a copy of the invoice directly, then I'll call you later to make an agreement about the payment."

e) "That's a shame. So that's the reason! I'm glad that it's nothing more serious; so we can arrange it as soon as possible."

f) "I'll send a copy immediately. Then I'll call you tomorrow and we can come to an agreement on how and when payment is to be made?"

g) "Oh, no! Let's ensure that nothing else can go wrong! How should we address invoices?"

As an excuse, this counter-argument is in fact a very bad one, the impediment thrown up is too simple to solve in the short term.

Always strive to get a complete copy of the invoice on the customer's desk as soon as possible, and make concrete agreements about payment immediately!

You should also always assure yourself that invoices will be sent in the same manner in the future, so that the same problem does not occur again nor can that particular excuse be used again. Have the debtor propose the correct address (department etc.).

8. The payment is on the way
This is the best news a credit manager can hear! If it is true...

This is why this remark is included in the counter-arguments because it isn't always that simple.

To be able to check the claim, it is important that you be well informed about the exact details of the money transfer. Then we know where and when we can expect which amount.

a) "Fantastic! When did you transfer it? OK... then we have our money...... it'll be with us about this Friday! Thanks very much!"

b) "Ah, that's what I like to hear! To which account number did you make the transfer? I'll ensure that the transaction is processed directly on arrival."

c) "Perfect. Exactly which invoice(s) are concerned? Can you give me the check number so that I can call my bank?"

d) "That's good news. Could you perhaps verify for me when the amount was transferred? Then I can take it into account."

All responses boil down to trying to discover what can be expected the amount, the invoice, the method of payment and the date.

The date is especially important. Always give a reasonable date by which the money must be received, and have it approved by the debtor. You will then always be left with a substantial lever if payment remains outstanding and the debtor has to be subsequently confronted.

9. Payment went wrong

It is human to err, but credit managers often become distrustful of repeated errors. It is possible for someone to fill in a wrong account number, forget to sign a credit transfer form or forget to state an amount. This isn't the best excuse in the book, unless it is the intention to pay as soon as possible. Someone who says that the fault is in the credit transfer acknowledges that the payment has to be made, end of discussion. The goods/services delivered and the invoice were therefore entirely satisfactory! The debtor can no longer call upon any other counter-arguments not to pay.

a) "How annoying. What went wrong exactly?"

b) "Oh. But I assume that the problem has been resolved?"

c) "Well yes, that can happen. I'm pleased in any case that you've already paid. When can I expect the amount from you?"

d) "Ah! Can I help to find the problem and to solve it?"

e) "To which account number did you transfer the money?"

f) "What was the amount you transferred exactly? Exactly which invoice(s) were concerned?

g) "It's only human to make mistakes. Have you already made the payment again? To which account number? How much? When?"

10. Something not in order with product/services/invoice

Although it might not seem important, as it involves just one description, a complaint or dispute occupies an exceptionally weighty position in the spectrum of counter-arguments. A complaint is annoying, not only because it delays payment, but in particular because it concerns a dissatisfied customer!

The same communication techniques that have been discussed earlier can be used with complaints. That means that we first "endorse" the explanations provided by the customer. This involves *letting the customer become aware that you are listening, taking them seriously and being sympathetic!*

In many cases customers will react angrily. The key to good customer relations is to demonstrate understanding for the customer's *feelings and emotions,* even though you disagree with the *content* of the complaint.

a) "I can imagine that you feel that way......"

b) "I completely understand your reaction...."

c) "Very understandable that you are disappointed..."

In actual fact, by adopting a position alongside the customer, their anger is dissipated and an atmosphere of mutuality is created. The first irritations are cushioned; now is the time to examine them with the customer and see if they are valid!

d) "You just said…. Could you explain that again please?"

e) "I don't understand…..completely. Could you give me an example?"

By talking about the problem, the level of irritation will gradually diminish. Slowly direct the conversation away from emotions and feelings and limit it to *facts*. The aim is to engage in a rational discussion, in which you and the customer can analyze how reasonable the complaint is. In the meantime make comprehensive notes on the actual nature of the complaint!

In most cases, the credit manager is not the appropriate person for actually solving a valid complaint. What they can do is place the complaint with the correct party within the organization. Good knowledge of internal procedures, routings, those responsible and products or services is therefore essential; a good credit manager is after all in a central position, and has extensive contact with various other departments.

Make comprehensive and clear notes of the complaint and tell the customer that you will personally ensure that the matter will be dealt with as soon as possible. That means: that someone from the company will contact the customer, *and not vice versa!*

f) "Unfortunately I cannot do anything about it, our Service department will call you back today."

g) "That is indeed a matter that must be put right, Mr. Williams. I will ensure that our Ms. Jones calls you back today, and she will be able to help you further!"

h) "Most annoying that this could happen. I will ensure that someone will come and look at the complaint by tomorrow at the latest. When can we call you for an appointment?"

In chapter 3, we demonstrated that the trick was to provide the customer with a clear opportunity to make their complaints known during the transaction cycle. After all, the customer will have to pay eventually, complaint or no complaint! The seriousness of the complaint determines the way in which to deal with it. If the complaint is in your opinion very serious, you can say for example:

i) "Your complaint has priority. I'll connect you through immediately. We'll talk to each other again when it has been solved."

j) "As soon as this situation has been solved, I will contact you to make an arrangement about payment."

If, however, you are of the opinion that the complaint, which may be frivolous, should not get in the way of payment, another angle of approach should be taken. You can challenge the reasonableness of the complaint:

94

k) "It's a great pity that you waited so long to report the complaint."

l) "Actually, you should have claimed after 8 days, not after 60 days. We do want to help you, but then you must insure that this invoice is paid as soon as possible!"

The point to be made from the outset is that if a complaint is first being voiced to the credit manager, too long a period of time has already gone by. If the supplier ensures that clear rules have been recorded in their general terms and conditions with regard to claims and submitting complaints, the credit manager can make this point effectively.

By giving the customer several opportunities to make their displeasure known, a steadily greater part of the "blame" for the non-payment can be attributed to the customer.

If the complaint is eventually resolved satisfactorily, payment should occur as soon as possible. A satisfactory resolution provides the credit manager with a comfortable point of departure;

n) "That was solved quickly, wasn't it. Can we expect the payment just as quickly?"

o) "I see here that your problem has been solved. Are you satisfied? That's good, could we then make an arrangement about the bill, because it is now...... old!"

p) "If you had warned us earlier, it wouldn't have gotten so out of hand. The same thing applies to the invoice, when can we expect to see the payment?"

Although it is not often seen as such, a complaint – certainly a valid complaint – is a chance for a company to benefit in terms of repaired customer relations. The first condition for a potential benefit is that the company must have the intention to deal with a complaint as quickly and thoroughly as possible and not to try to avoid it. The second condition is that the company must be prepared to learn from a complaint.

What is ultimately better than being able to demonstrate to the customer that your company is able and in a position to respond to unexpected situations decisively and in a customer-orientated manner?

A properly handled complaint makes for the best customer loyalty!

The "golden rules" for receiving and dealing with a complaint are set out below:

- Take every complaint seriously
- Remain calm and contained, even if the customer is not
- Respond with understanding to the customer's **emotions and feelings**
- Never be directly defensive (remember, you didn't ship the product personally)
- Respond objectively and critically to the **facts**
- Place the complaint in the correct location in the organization.
- Never hide behind another department
- The customer is called back, and not vice versa
- Clearly tell the customer what they can expect
- Check whether the complaint has been resolved then contact the customer once again

11. We have other payment arrangements
Some companies have specific payment policies that structure their payments to outside suppliers. That is not to say that these should be accepted without question! In principle the suppler has two options with which to respond:

1. Adjust the price
2. Try to change the payment behavior

96

A delayed payment costs the supplier money. If the terms of payment applied by a specific customer are well known beforehand, the price can be adjusted accordingly. Whether this is a desirable approach will have to be assessed by each company; this option does not fall under "telephone collection", and will not be further discussed.

The second option is an awkward one. Nevertheless, there are still a few good responses for a credit manager:

a) "I understand that you operate a different payment system, but our price is based on payment terms of ......days. We would gladly like to remain in a position to be able to offer such an attractive price!"

b) "Actually I don't understand. We don't tell you that we are suddenly going to deliver on another day, do we? Don't you think it would simply be better if we both fulfil our agreements?"

c) "I quite understand, but your payment conditions are really not applicable to this delivery, for which your company has signed."

d) "Oh? Could you tell me with who the amended agreement was made?"

e) "You are a bit late. The contract is clear that you honor our conditions, and I don't understand why you now suddenly come back to that."

f) "It's annoying that this alternate agreement is not in writing. I only have your signature under a contract with *our* terms".

Once again the immense importance of good general terms and conditions becomes evident in these examples.

12. Have not had time
This counter-argument is definitely the ultimate example of "indifference". It is not a question of *time*, but of *priority*. Apparently the other party finds other matters more important than paying your bill. This happens frequently, so it is a considerable problem:

a) "So business is good! Perhaps we could also benefit?"

b) "It is clear to me that you're busy, but if you could arrange payment immediately, then you'll have one thing less to do!"

c) "I realize that, but since we're on the telephone anyway, wouldn't it be more efficient to arrange it quickly now?"

d) "If you could just make the payment, I won't have to disturb you again!"

e) "Busy, busy, busy...... I understand, but since I have already drawn your attention to this overdue item, I think it would be more useful if you paid it immediately!"

f) "Do you know what? In .....days a few other invoice dates will expire. What would you say if I gave you all the details now so that they can all be paid in one shot? Then you'll have one less worry to contend with!"

13. Forgetting
We all forget sometimes. In this case your strongest powers of persuasion are not needed to arrange the payment:

a) "So you see it was good that I called!"

b) "Well let's go, you can make it up by paying today!"

98

c) "Oh, I didn't disturb you for nothing then. I trust that you will put everything in order immediately?"

d) "Oh, but I certainly didn't forget you!"

e) "That happens to me too sometimes. Could you arrange it today then?"

f) "That's possible. Could you do me a favor and transfer the payment today?"

Forgetting is human and it often provides a good opportunity for injecting some humor into the situation and arriving at a better relationship with the customer!

They who always pay far too late, will one day go bankrupt
(Old banking rule)

14. We have no money

A debtor with liquidity problems: the nightmare of every credit manager! Imagine that the company is going bankrupt, how great is the damage that we will suffer...

The most important thing to do is to ascertain the seriousness of the situation. This means a thorough re-examination of the situation; how it has occurred, how serious it actually is and what the outlook is. In addition, it is advisable to request a credit report (from Graydon) that will provide you with insight into the current situation, independent of other advice.

Some internal discussion within your company is warranted at this juncture. The situation must be reported to Sales, to the person with the ultimate responsibility for credit management. In mutual consultation, you must quickly decide how to deal with this debtor.

Whether it is a win-win or a win-lose situation, in each case other possible payment arrangements must be properly considered, in addition to examining how to proceed with current or future orders. The appropriate procedures will be discussed in the following chapter.

A COMPANY WITHOUT MONEY DOES NOT EXIST!

Find the money! Every company has money, only they may not have any money for you! As soon as a company experiences liquidity problems, the creditors are paid in order of importance. Usually employees, the Inland Revenue, the trade association, social security contributions and the bank. In addition to these the secured and unsecured creditors, including suppliers must be satisfied. This usually includes paying the suppliers important to the continuation of the company and then those creditors that threaten to scream loudest...

If you can, make alternate arrangements, obtain guarantees; ask for partial payments...get something. You never know whether the company will survive or whether you will find yourself in a long line of creditors.

A good credit manager has to ensure that his company is classified as a priority on the debtor's list. That can only be achieved by remaining reasonable and making a feasible proposal (see the following chapter: Negotiation).

A number of examples of possible responses are provided below, that which can be chosen according to the point of departure taken by the supplier: win – win or win – lose:

a) "That's not so good. Could you tell me some more about it?"

b) "Oh dear. How did that happen? Do you have any idea how long it will last?"

c) "I can imagine that every company is sometimes a bit strapped for cash. Can you propose a solution?"

d) "It's a shame that you had to involve us by making an order while you knew that you couldn't pay."

e) "Same with us. That's why I'm calling!"

f) ...... PAUSE ...... "How do you think we're going to solve this?"

g) ......: PAUSE ...... "Why is it that you don't have any money?"

h) "That seems to me to be all the more reason to pay this bill. Otherwise it'll cost even more money......"

i) "What is the name and telephone number of the receiver?"

j) "Now, now, it can't be that bad. You're still being paid aren't you?"

k) "It can't be very pleasant working with that hanging over your head. What exactly do you mean by 'no money'?"

l) "That's not so good. What exactly does that mean for us?"

Remember, this may be the time to be creative. Ask first what they suggest but have a back-up plan. Time will be of the essence in these situations. Make sure your management can accept an alternative. Consider a set-off or accepting their product as payment. Whatever it takes unless you are able to sustain the loss.

Again, your responses should follow the path indicated below, in any of these situations:

1. Endorsement
- Interest
- Sympathy

2. Continuing questioning
- problem
- cause
- consequence
- duration
- seriousness

3. Check authenticity
- Solution?
- Action taken by the debtor
- Action that we can undertake ourselves

4. Solution
- Advantage for the debtor

Conclusion

Counter-arguments must always be taken seriously, even if you are convinced that they are nothing more than an excuse not to pay. You should be the designer and arbiter of the eventual outcome of the conversation. Getting paid!

Complaints need not be entirely negative. If you succeed in handling them in an appropriate and correct manner, complaints can work to your advantage. Customers can be angry and emotive; a natural response and it is nothing to fear. Show understanding for *emotions and feelings* but talk about the *facts* of the matter.

REGISTER EXACTLY WHAT THE CUSTOMER TELLS YOU: THIS GIVES YOU THE OPPORTUNITY TO RETURN TO THIS LATER AND TO CHECK WHETHER A CERTAIN CUSTOMER IS CONSISTENT!

TAKE THE OPPORTUNITY TO TALK WITH COLLEAGUES IN OTHER CREDIT DEPARTMENTS. ASK THEM ABOUT GOOD OPENING LINES AND PHRASES. LET THEM TELL YOU WHEN AND WHERE THEY HAVE BEEN SUCCESSFUL!

MAKE A SMALL LIST OF GOOD RESPONSES TO COUNTER-ARGUMENTS AND ALWAYS KEEP IT CLOSE AT HAND!

ASK YOUR OWN ACCOUNTS PAYABLE DEPARTMENT WHAT LINES GET THEM TO PAY AND INCLUDE THEM IN YOUR REPERTOIRE.

Having is having, but getting is the trick......

7.   NEGOTIATING

Ne•go•ti•ate (past part. negotiated) discuss something in order to reach an agreement; **Ne•go•ti•a•tion** *n* (-s)

"It's our money, we have a right to it, you'd better pay!" If only it were that simple. I'll simply call them up, ask for the money, I'm right they'll pay. If it truly were this easy, we wouldn't be writing this book. The credit manager will often have to enter into negotiations to reach an agreement. Negotiation means; giving and taking, giving and making concessions.

You need to become not only an effective communicator but also an effective negotiator to succeed at your chosen profession.

The structure of a collection conversation was described in chapter 5 with the following elements:

1. Introduction
2. Information phase
3. Agreement
4. Summary
5. Conclusion

Another part of the conversation could be inserted between the information phase and the agreement, the negotiation phase:

1.   Introduction
2.   Information phase
3.   Negotiation

4. Agreement
5. Summary
6. Conclusion

Many people view it as irksome that they are forced to negotiate a contract that was signed with fixed terms and conditions after their part of the bargain has been fulfilled. Reality is a cruel reminder that no contract is ever ironclad until you are PAID!

Once the seller has negotiated with the customer to get the order, it would appear to be up to the credit manager to ensure, via further negotiation, that the sale comes full circle.

Accordingly, as long as the customer still requires goods and service from your company and you require continued sales to that customer, the credit manager has a responsibility to ensure that the transaction cycle is and remains acceptable for both parties.

The word "negotiation" suggests that the stated terms and conditions will not be adhered to but that we will have to be content with less. For the credit manager an optimum result means: immediate and full payment by a highly satisfied customer.

The objectives to strive for can be divided into three parts:
• Full payment
• Immediate payment
• Continued Customer Satisfaction

Since negotiation is a question of give and take, it means that the credit manager will reach his objective on certain points and not on others. Full payment for example, but not immediate. Or full payment, but a dissatisfied customer......

A good negotiating position begins with **information**. Knowledge is power. The person who is aware of all the relevant details concerning the subject of the negotiation will command a strong position and not be easily caught unawares.

What information is important?

106

- The basic data
  - Invoice information
  - Outstanding balance
  - Age of debt(s)

- The history
  - Previous agreements
  - Complaints
  - Experience of previous transactions

The positioning phase also belongs with the information phase. The credit manager must define an objective in advance. KNOW FROM THE OUTSET WHAT IT IS YOU WANT TO ACCOMPLISH.

- Why are we calling?
- What is the objective?
  - → an outstanding unpaid account
  - → an unacceptable pattern or payment behavior
- What is our choice of strategy?
- Where do we want to go with this customer?
  - → in the short term
  - → in the distant future

Some objectives are more important than others. During the preparation stage it is not only necessary to establish what objectives are to be achieved, but also what concessions can be made. Identify areas where your company can be flexible.

In addition, a good negotiator will place themselves in the other person's position. By pausing to consider the possible objectives of the other party, you can better estimate the advantages to be gained and the concessions that must be made.

The negotiator should try and answer the questions below prior to every negotiation. The answers will help you to be fully prepared.

1. What do you and your company want to achieve?
2. What does the debtor want?
3. What are the common points of departure?
4. What limits that I can accept?
5. What concessions can I make?
6. What proposals can I make in order to solve the problem?
7. With what approach shall I conduct the conversation?

A good negotiator will finish closer to their own objectives and will have to make fewer concessions!

Negotiation: the technique (1)

Negotiation is an art, a subtle game of give and take and of carefully sounding out the other party. Anyone can learn it!

The big trick in negotiation is stating your final position as late in the conversation as possible. That means: give the initiative to the other party and wait as long as possible to make your proposal.

Everyone knows the saying: 'Start high, end low'. It is however much better not to stake anything at all, let alone high. The example below illustrates this tactic:

Peter is on holiday and wants to buy a bracelet on the beach. He only has 10 dollars left. The seller bought the bracelets for 2 dollars and wants a minimum of 4 dollars for each of them.

Peter is a smart lad and wants to haggle:

"I'll give you 6 dollars tops for it!"

From that moment the seller already has a potential 4 dollars in profit. He is already 2 dollars above his minimum profit price. And it can only get better:

"No way Mister! It's not worth my while, I'll be running around the whole day for nothing and then I can't go home because what will my ten hungry kids say!"

Of course Peter had not expected it to be so easy:

"OK, but I won't give more than 8 dollars for it!"

The seller counts another 2 dollars to his profit and sees what else can be achieved:

"8 dollars? For such a lovely bracelet?! You can do better than that, you're practically stealing it from me!"

Peter is getting nervous, as he is now coming close to his limit. He tries again:

"9 dollars, that's my last offer. "I'm not going any higher!"

The seller is again a dollar richer and decides to sell. Peter is content that he has earned something, but the seller is obviously the most satisfied!

An entirely different exchange could have taken place:

Peter is on holiday and wants to buy a bracelet on the beach. He only has 10 dollars left. The seller bought the bracelets for 2 dollars and wants a minimum of 4 dollars for each of them.

Peter is a smart lad and wants to haggle:
"How much does the bracelet cost?"

The seller is not happy with that. That is exactly what he doesn't want:

"How much do you have to give?"

Peter does not let himself be softened up:

"No, I asked you how much the bracelet costs. What is the price?"

The seller thinks, play high stakes:
"10 dollars."

Peter now knows that the armband is within his limit. The first gain!
"10 dollars for this! Ridiculous! Never! Robbery!"

The seller still has room for maneuver:

"OK, as it's you, special price for a Dutchman: 8 dollars."

And Peter has earned his first 2 dollars. But he still is not satisfied:

"Do I look that stupid? A bracelet like this is never worth 8 dollars!"

The seller is still a way from his limit and therefore can drop a little further:

"As the weather is so nice, an extra special price: 6 dollars:

It's going well for Peter; he's now 4 dollars below his limit. Just a quick look to see whether there is more of a discount to be had:

"I don't think that's such a special price!"

Peter then turns round and pretends that he's about to walk away. The seller quickly makes another offer:

"Since I have to eat as well, and even though I'm earning hardly anything out of it: 5 dollars!"

Peter comes back and buys the bracelet.

The wisdom of waiting before you adopt a firm position appears clear from the above examples. From the moment a position has been taken, the target has been defined and will have to be defended. From that moment onwards it can only get worse. The only way to still come out of it reasonably is to start from an almost untenable starting point, but there is then the risk that that will cause irritation to the other party. The other party will then gain the impression that they are being pressured and that there is no room for maneuver or for a reasonable and open negotiation.

Lesson one for the negotiator is:

Let the other party make the first proposal

That can be achieved by:

Asking an open-ended question!

Some examples are:

a) What are your thoughts on solving the problem?
b) What is your proposal?
c) What are your options?

You can then weigh the answer that you are given and accept or decline. Avoid making a counter proposal too early in the game. Let them, adjust their initial; bid and work from that point.

Negotiation: the technique (2)

Making concessions is a part of most negotiations. The manner in which concession is arrived at is even more important than the concession itself: a concession need not be an entire capitulation.

By agreeing with the other party's proposal we allow for the fact that they have won something. At that moment the other party is pleased, and the negotiator must make take advantage of this momentary satisfaction. This is done by coupling a ***marginal condition*** to the concession. We call that the "Yes, but......."

For example, you are prepared to agree to the payment of half the debt, but you want the money immediately:

"It is acceptable that you pay half of the amount for the time being, but only under the condition that we receive it by tomorrow morning!"

By applying the "Yes, but" approach you know for certain that you will get something back for every concession. In that manner you do not have to worry that you give too much away and get too little in return!

The technique is exceptionally suitable for making future agreements. By showing a degree of flexibility, you can provide for better payment behavior from the debtor in the future. Ultimately one of the most important objectives that the credit manager strives for: the overall structural improvement of their debtor's payment behavior!

Perhaps it sounds a bit strange, but in a certain sense the fact that a debtor pays late is an opportunity for the future. The debtor knows perfectly well that they are in the wrong, and at the moment that you appear flexible to them, they are placed under an obligation to you. That obligation can be used to correct their behavior in the future.

a) Good, lets do it your way this time, but you have to realize that this is an absolute exception; in the future your company will also have to stick to the rules of the game!"

b) Ok. I'll agree to your proposal, but only on the condition you must promise our invoices will be paid on time in the future."

Negotiation: the technique (3)

During negotiations, both partys' proposals shift up and down, with the objective of eventually reaching an outcome acceptable to everyone. The decision whether or not to agree with a certain proposal often rests on the manner in which it is has been presented; how it is packaged.

If, for example, you put an argument forward that payment is far too late:

1. Payment is already a month late!
2. The invoice is already two months old!

It is clear that the second remark has greater impact than the first. The formulation of the message or proposal has significant impact on the perception that you want to create. In the following example, we have a debtor with consecutive outstanding balances:

Not late	$ 6,000
00 – 30 days late	$ 8,000
31 – 60 days late	$ 2,500
61 – 90 days late	$ 1,500

Imagine from the outset that you want to have the oldest amount paid at all costs and that anything over 30 days really should be paid ($4,000). The debtor proposes to pay the oldest amount of $1,500.

By placing this amount in perspective with the total outstanding balance, you can appeal to the reasonableness of the other party:

"$1,500? That doesn't really put a dent in the total outstanding balance of $18,000?"

The initiative is now with them to respond to this open-ended, highly suggestive question and to come back with another, more realistic proposal!

Negotiation: general instructions, tips and techniques
1. Prepare yourself thoroughly and systematically.
2. Do you have all the relevant information at your disposal?
3. Is your boss 100% behind you?
4. Determine the most important objectives.
5. Establish the minimum and maximum requirements.
6. What concessions can you make?
7. What marginal conditions do you want to include with the concessions?
8. Have you established whether your contact person is authorized to conduct negotiations?
9. Think of how you are going to present it to the customer.
10. Where do you want to finish with the customer?
11. Approach and content are two totally different matters. You can be a tough negotiator without being unpleasant or unfriendly.
12. Do not be afraid of a stalemate. Impasses can always be broken down.
13. Never make concessions immediately. Wait.
14. Do not try to make an offer too soon. Let the other party go first.
15. Negotiate as an equal not as a supplicant.
16. First discuss the matters that are fairly easy to resolve, this creates a positive atmosphere of trust; a good basis for the rest of the negotiation.
17. Gather all proposals before formulating your response.
18. Remain friendly.
19. Only make agreements that are really acceptable for both parties. Unattainable propositions do not deliver a thing!
20. Regularly ask probing questions to be certain that there is no miscommunication.

Negotiation: companies with liquidity problems
Negotiations with companies that have liquidity problems are slightly more difficult because you always have to make more concessions than you would like to. The situation compels us to go a long way to accommodate the customer.

Where at all possible, the customer should make the first move: they will have to show their good will in solving the problem. If a debtor is unprepared in finding a solution, they do not deserve your assistance. In these instances, a win – lose situation has presented itself militating in favor of going directly to the collection agency...

114

Most negotiations with a company that is experiencing liquidity problems concern an attainable and realistic payment arrangement. A payment arrangement is realistic if it provides attainable payments by offering both the debtor and supplier a viable option for the eventual reimbursement of the debt.

Minimum components of a payment arrangement:

• The total debt
• Interest percentage and amount
• Expiry date
• Installments
• Installment amounts
• Method of payment
• Penalties

The payment arrangement expires the moment it is not fulfilled. Compliance should be very strictly enforced through regular contact with the debtor, even when things are going well!

To avoid problems arising with compliance concerning payment arrangements, it is better to choose smaller amounts over short periods of time. Many payment problems arise through a company leaving small amounts open for too long, resulting in these suddenly becoming large amounts that consequently cannot be paid off in a single installment. It is therefore better to opt for $100 a week than for $400 a month. In addition, shorter periods also allow you to monitor compliance with the arrangement more effectively!

Key points with payment arrangements:
• Always confirm arrangements in writing
• An arrangement only takes effect when customer has signed for it
• Preference for smaller amounts
• Preference for shorter periods
• Have your contact person's manager sign the approval
• Have your own manager and/or responsible party in your company sign the approval
• Distribute copies of the arrangement internally to those concerned

Negotiation: win – lose

Finally, negotiating with customer that we are willing to cut off unless they pay up immediately. The win – lose scenario remains a setback for your company. Ultimately the loss of a customer has occurred, even if it is a customer who has caused more trouble than profit. The pattern of a win – lose conversation constitutes in making it clear to the customer that this is really the last time that they will be given the opportunity to meet their obligations. **There is no going back on that decision!**

In this instance, the willingness of the credit manager to make concessions has disappeared. There are two options: the debtor pays the debt or legal action is taken.

A win – lose negotiation begins by making it clear to the debtor *why* this final discussion is taking place. This means a detailed review of the opportunities that were given for payment, the agreements, which have not been fulfilled, and the promises that have not been kept.

Prior to this conversation the credit manager should communicate and discuss his/her decision internally. Sales, customer service and management must be in agreement with the decision. Regardless of the credit manager's authority, it is always worthwhile to touch base with the experience of others in this respect, thereby ensuring that everyone is absolutely convinced that an actual win – lose situation exists.

A win – lose negotiation consists of the following elements:

1. Clearly give the reasons why demands are being made:
   - Recount the behavior of the customer
   - Restate the measures that you have taken: flexibility, patience, arrangements etc.
   - Indicate what your company policy is with respect to these matters

2. Clearly indicate what demands are being made

3. Make it unequivocally clear that these demands are final

4. Make it unequivocally clear what the consequences are

5. Conclusion:
   • Briefly repeat what is now expected from the customer
   • Repeat which steps you are taking.
   • Express your expectations

Conclusion
Negotiation remains an enormously interesting and exiting part of the work of a credit manager! By frequently practicing and consciously analyzing your negotiating conversation skills, you will soon understand your strengths and weaknesses and will make considerable progress managing the accounts that are in your charge!

A good negotiator succeeds in obtaining a maximum result from a pleasant conversation, and knows how to limit to an absolute minimum the damage of an already frayed relationship. Negotiating can be the most exiting and enjoyable part of the work of the credit manager. In no other area will you be able to shine from both a customer service standpoint and a debt recuperation standpoint!

IF THERE IS ONE AREA WHERE A DEFINITIVE PROFITS CAN SURFACE, THEN IT IS IN NEGOTIATIONS WITH CUSTOMERS!

NEGOTIATION MEANS THAT YOU MUST BE PREPARED TO MAKE CONCESSIONS!

A compromise is the trick of cutting the cake in such a manner that everyone thinks that they are getting the largest slice

8. INTERNATIONAL COLLECTION CALLS

One of the key elements to successful international collections is preparation. The more homework you have done in advance of the call or the collection, the higher your success rate will be and the more efficiently your precious resources will be allocated.

This chapter attempts to give some guidelines on preparing for an international collection and succeeding in getting paid by a foreign buyer.

One of the best defenses is a good offense. This could not be truer than in the international context where preparation is everything. Not only will you avoid future headaches but also you will undoubtedly save your company some money in the long run.

Remember you have distance, a foreign legal system, a linguistic barrier and a different business culture to deal with so why make your job any harder than it has to be? Setting up a set of procedures and guidelines for managing international receivables is an onerous task but one that will pay off in saved time and money in the long run. In addition, you will learn something about new systems and business and legal cultures. It may be fun- that's up to you.

Collection Letters:
Using the mail for international collections has its evident downside. Other than the invoices that you have already sent to the purchaser, the collection letter may appear to be an idle threat. Do not wait for it to work. As backup documentation, a letter should be sent to the appropriate party once you have determined that payment is not forthcoming but this should not delay your calls to the delinquent debtor.

Patience:
As discussed later in this chapter under the heading: "Time", the term or period given to pay an invoice is perceived in many varied ways. From the outset, a credit manager should be a little more patient with international accounts. This does not translate into being inactive but simply in realizing that in certain places the pace is more relaxed. If you factor this into the credit equation from the outset, your planning will be more accurate and your ulcers less aggressive.

The Proper Party:
Have you identified the appropriate person who is responsible for the payment? Communicating with the wrong party can waste significant resources from both a time and monetary perspective. Your international credit application should have determined who is responsible for what in a particular company. Calling a clerk 100 times will get you nowhere, whereas one call to a director may solve the problem

Humor is one of the hardest linguistic elements to master. While you may think you are being unbelievably witty and clever, the party at the other end of the line may at best have simply ignored your clever quip or at worst been completely offended.

Speak Clearly
If you have ever attempted to learn another language, you will have appreciated someone speaking clearly and slowly in their native tongue. While you might be quite capable in a classroom setting, speaking with someone who has a different accent than the one you originally learned can be defeating.

If you apply this logic to your telephone counterpart located in country X, you may find that you will be helping them out significantly and avoiding confusion. Remember they do not necessarily work in English and may need a little practice. While the conversation may be slow, you'll avoid repetition, misunderstanding and general confusion.

Speak slowly not louder
By the same token, as noted earlier in this book, the temptation when you are not being understood is to raise the level of your

voice. This of course, isn't going to help. Try to monitor yourself when you are calling overseas. Does your voice mysteriously increase in decibels?

Do not use idioms or slang. "That's *one way to skin a cat*" may have an entirely different meaning in countries with varied culinary menus. You may end up with a shipment of cat as a set-off against the price of your shipped goods. Again, idiomatic language, much like humor falls into the realm of the strange and incomprehensible to a non-native speaker- Avoid it!

Have your documentation in order and back up papers in front of you. The more you can accomplish in one call without having to rummage around to look for the appropriate order or contract, the better your success rate will be. As you refer to invoices, dates and the like, their immediate accessibility will make you appear more confident and in control.

If absolutely necessary, you can fax copies of the referenced material to the buyer if they need the material to follow the conversation. Remember, this creates more time, expense and methods of avoidance *(Oh. We never got that fax)*. They should already have all of the documentation that you have.

Schedule the call. Take sometime out of your day to make this call if it is important. Avoid interruptions. Scheduling the call with the other party, however, depends on your relationship with them. It is always easy to put someone off to another time. Schedule once but after that try spur of the moment calls.

Mobile phone. Most executives around the world have mobile telephones that go with them everywhere. One of the best methods of reaching your intended party is to call them on their mobile phone. There is no receptionist and no one to screen their calls. You may also get them at a moment where they will be surprised and not be able to think of an excuse for why they haven't paid in 190 days.

Include a space in your international credit application for mobile numbers and personal home phone numbers. Calling people at home is not advised unless you are aware of the particular jurisdiction's laws on collection calls.

Guarantees:
Refer to any and all of the guarantees that you may have. If you have in your possession a pagare (promissory note) signed by the director of the company, make use of its strategic power. Refer to it and if you are not speaking to the party who has provided the personal guarantee, make them aware that one has been given.

These instruments are excellent strategic tools in the payment game.

Background:
Know something about the country you where your debtor is located. If you can make a comment on the economic or political scene in a particular region you are sending two messages:

1. That you are sophisticated about world issues
2. And most importantly that you have shown some interest in that party's home and situation.

People love to talk about their countries and their lives. Make neutral comments, avoid partisan opinions. You never know whose cousin is leader of the opposition or the outgoing dictator. Listen and ask them questions, this may help your overall credit perception of the country in general and allow you to get important information on your client.

If, for instance, you had called on a Mexican company following the peso devaluation in 1995 without taking into account the drop in the value of the currency and asked them to pay you immediately, you might have been in for a shock. Most foreign corporations who did get paid following the Mexican devaluation where those who stayed in close contact with their buyers and made arrangements for the repayment of the debts outstanding. Immediate contact with the buyer demonstrated their concern and understanding of the situation but also showed that they would be on top of the accounts regardless of the economic future. The Mexican company received the signal that they would have to pay no matter what at some point in the future.

In a situation as draconian as a devaluation and depending on the volume of receivables, a personal visit would be recommended over a telephone call.

Do not use first names:
In most countries around the world, the use of a surname is recommended. Starting out a conversation with a perfect stranger by using their first name is viewed as presumptuous and overly familiar; in some countries it is insulting. Wait until you are asked by the other party to address them by their first name.

On the other side of the coin, if you need to make an impact and are not overly concerned about future relations with the particular client. The use of a first name may be warranted. It should not be resorted to lightly.

Business as an extension of personality:
In many nations, the concept of business is tightly interwoven with personal relations. In Asia, the concept of "face" and the occasional saving of said "face" is quite important. In Latin America, your personal relationship with the trading partner may be vital to your success in any aspect of the transaction.

How does this affect your ability to collect. Sometimes, if the numbers warrant or the other approaches are futile, you may wish to have the person in your company who has the relationship with the buyer call them directly. In the corporate food chain that is your company, this may be extremely difficult but if it is possible it may yield dividends.

In countries where the business relationship is personal, you, the credit executive, who may never have seen the buyer, are extremely easy to ignore. On the other hand, your company's representative who probably sat down and ate a meal with the buyer or asked about their children is not as easy to brush off. In fact, it may be quite shaming to get a call from this particular individual.

In the alternative, if there is no way that you can have your company's representative call the buyer directly, for whatever reason, ask them if you can use their name.

During the course of the conversation with the slow payer refer to your company representative's name, refer to the time they may have spent with the debtor, get details. Drag the conversation kicking and screaming into the realm of the personal. At this point, you are harder to ignore.

Titles:
Titles are important in many countries. If you want to get off on the right foot from the beginning, address the person by their title if they have one. For example if you are calling a German client, he or she will be pleased to be addressed as Doctor if they have received the requisite degree of higher education. Failing to use their title may put them on the defensive or simply make them dismiss what it is you are really trying to accomplish.

"*I'm suing you!*" is not an appropriate greeting:
In less litigious societies, (most of the rest of the world), people and businesses do not use the courts as an all-purpose and daily dispute resolution mechanism. In some countries threatening litigation can have dire consequences for the party making the threat. While litigation is often a necessary or viable option, unless you are familiar with the laws of that country stay away from the threat. Instead, say that you will refer the matter to counsel.

Moreover, in some countries (India for example) the court system is so clogged that your claim may wait ten years prior to adjudication. Corruption of the judiciary may also be a problem. The concept to be aware of in this case that suing someone in a foreign jurisdiction may not provide the result that you originally were seeking and instead may be the cause of further delays and problems.

Avoid finishing their sentences:
This is one of the great temptations when speaking to anyone who does not completely master your language. You assume that you know what it is they want to say and can completely direct a conversation. Wait and let the person struggle through what it is they wish to communicate., By finishing someone sentences you may leave with one impression while they are operating under a completely different set of ideas. Moreover, they may not understand what it is you have

said and will simply say yes to terminate the conversation as quickly as possible.

Your enemy the ringer:
In some countries calls from outside the national borders ring in a different tone. If someone is avoiding your calls and can tell from the outset that the call is not domestic, have an local associate or a distributor call them for you.

This tactic may have the dual effect of linguistic clarity and circumventing foreign call avoidance.

Have an international credit application:
Your company should have one or more international credit applications to be used with non-US parties. The laws differ throughout the world and you may be able to obtain far more information in some countries than you would at home. Take advantage of this and find out as much as you can about your buyer. Remember that they will be using your money for whatever the terms of the credit you give them; are you not entitled to some information?

In addition to the credit application, a proper credit report or credit check should accompany any granting of credit to a foreign entity. The task of collecting is already difficult enough without operating on misinformation from the outset of the transaction. Many companies have granted credit to existing businesses only to find out that these businesses were never legal entities in their domestic markets.

A complete credit report will give you information not only on the company and its management and director's but will alert you to any legal danger signs that may impede your future collections efforts. Your ability to access this information may be hampered after a problem has occurred; A credit report should be obtained and be part of your policy at the beginning of the credit process.

Periodic review of your accounts is also recommended. Your credit reporting company should have a reminder system in place to alert you of the accounts that need updating.

Time:
In many countries around the globe, time is not particularly of the essence. Every region in world has their own concept of time and priority. The frantic pace of Europe and North America's business world is not shared by the rest of the globe's inhabitants and corporate citizens. What this translates into is that patience is required.

Moreover, prior to granting credit and making a credit decision, you should have some idea of the payment practices in a particular country. If for instance in country X net thirty will inevitable translate into 90 days, this calculation should be factored into your credit equation. In other words, grant 30 and not 60 but expect ninety.

Obtaining statistics from your industry group or from an international organization on country specific payment practices will inevitably help reduce anxiety and afford proper cash flow planning.

In country contact:
Do you have a contact in the country who is a native speaker and can call the non-payer on your behalf? If not, it may be time to go to an outside agency if you are not having any success.

Someone versed in the customs and business practices of a particular market will know the most appropriate and effective method of securing a payment. It may often be a personal contact or a perceived loss of face that will get you your money in the end. In-country payment resolution is always worth exploring.

Cost/time allocation:

One of the issues that should be addressed in any international sale and subsequent granting of credit is whether or not the credit department is best suited to pursue payment of the receivable. There are many facets of the transactions to contemplate prior to allocating the credit department's time and resources towards international collections.

Some of these include:

- Training in international credit & collections;
- Language barriers;
- Legal barriers;
- Lack of in-country presence;
- Estimation of time and associated costs for in-house overseas collections

It may be that you are an excellent domestic collector and probably would be an excellent overseas collector. You may not have the time, the training, the expertise, the linguistic ability, and the resources... to become an overseas collector. Prior to determining the best route for obtaining payment on the foreign receivables, it would be advisable that you sit down with management and determine what is the best method for allocating resources in this area.

If, for instance, you are using international sales as a market entry or a loss leader, the credit aspect of the transaction diminishes in importance. Management may say: *"Try your best and we'll deal with what we get."*

They may also say: *"We want full payment but we can afford to take a cut in margins."* This type of scenario may best be suited to a collection agency that has in-county contacts.

On the other side of the coin, your company's international sales may be vital to its bottom line. They might wish to fully train you in international credit and collections. They may want to have you deal only with the granting of credit and pass collections on to another agency

Another possibility is that the company can afford to purchase insurance for the international accounts, which may facilitate the credit function.

If cash flow is an issue for your company, you may wish to avail yourselves of the services of a factoring or forfeiting company to which you sell your receivables at a discount and collection, whether it be direct or on an underlying instrument, is organized by the third party company.

In sum, this is to say that there are many options open to the credit professional and that each of these should be taken into account when assessing whether or not your department is best suited to undertake the international collections effort.

Originals & Notarization:
In any material dealing with international transactions, the value of holding originals in your files should always be stressed. In many civil law jurisdictions around the world, Latin America; for example, you may not enter into evidence copies of originals without significant legal restrictions.

Having original documentation may be vital to your claim. In addition, if there are any questions of the validity of a document or if the document itself has a negotiable value (i.e. Promissory note or an equivalent pagare, for instance) it may be advisable to have this document notarized in the particular jurisdiction of origin.

Civil law jurisdictions are particularity fond of the concept of notarization to prove the validity of a document. If you are going to rely on a specific document to prove the your claim or title in a particular transaction, seeing a local notary may be wise.

Checklist:
- Do you have an international credit application?
- Do you know which party you want to contact?
- Do you know who to address if that contact fails (a superior) A chain of command?
- Do you have any additional guarantees for the payment of this account?
- Do you have a native speaker in your offices?
- Do you have an in-country contact?
- Do you have all of the paper work in front of you?
- Have you analyzed the cost effectiveness of making international collection calls yourself?
- Have you explored other alternatives

"Peace is saved, we have an agreement!"
(Chamberlain)

9. PUTTING IT ALL INTO PRACTICE

While this book provides many useful, practical and instructional tips that you can put to use the moment you step into the office, it remains only a bunch of words on paper unless you are willing to apply some of the techniques that have been discussed. As you become more willing to try implementing the approaches featured, the collection calls will start to become easier. The result should translate into more, successfully collected accounts.

This book has been compiled from the experiences of hundreds of credit managers and debt collection managers, every company is different, and every branch has its own rules, agreements and peculiarities... We recommend that you make as much use as possible of exchanging general experiences with your colleagues, both in your own company and with other credit people in your industry especially with international accounts, as this information is often harder to obtain on your own.

No one has a monopoly on wisdom, but everyone does have useful experiences or anecdotes. Credit Management is a profession, an enjoyable and fascinating profession, due not only to the contact with people but also because of the considerable business and operational facets to the job. As a result, the credit manager occupies an exceptional and central position within an organization.

Of course, every profession has its interesting side and its unpleasant aspects. Strangely enough, credit managers find telephone collection one of the less enjoyable parts of their work. While this may be true, the perceived negative can become a positive when the collection call is well mastered, it is a challenge that can deliver fantastic results!

Unfortunately a book remains nothing other than a bundle of theories. You can actually only improve your telephone skills by training and developing them in practice. A special training course, specifically intended for this purpose, has been developed by Graydon: The Telephone Collection Training Course. During the training course you are accompanied by a number of colleagues with whom you are intensively trained and counseled. The Telephone Collection Training Course also includes role-playing scenarios set in a variety of daily situations, which are consequently extensively analyzed and discussed under the guidance of an experienced trainer.

If you would like to participate in one of our training sessions or receive more information concerning these courses, please contact:

GRAYDON AMERICA INC.
Ms. Nancy Powell
116 John Street, Suite 3300
New York, NY 10038
1-630-942-5020
graydonamerica@mindspring.com

GRAYDON UK LTD.
Customer Services
Hyde House, Edgware Road
Colindale, London NW9 6LW
44-181-9751050
customerservices@graydon.co.uk

We sincerely hope that by reading this book, and possibly by participating in the training course, in the future you will be able to pick up the telephone with greater confidence and achieve better and positive results. Ultimately it all comes down to your ability to collect as efficiently and effectively as possible. We call that ability:

COLLECTION ABILITY!

Do business like a gypsy, but pay like a gentleman!
(Slavic expression)

Mañana is not an exotic drink!

EMILE VAN VEEN

Emile van Veen is the author of numerous articles and books on European credit and business, especially about the construction industry. Mr. Van Veen has held several management positions in the credit information division of Graydon Netherlands in Amsterdam. Now, using his expertise, he dedicates his time and energy to researching and writing. Emile is responsible for developing new marketing strategies and products for an affiliated company of the Graydon Group.

As author of *Graydon Ratios*, a tri-monthly, high profile scientific publication concerning economic developments in the Netherlands, he is further developing as a researcher. His passion, however, lies in writing about communications and business relations between people and putting those skills to professional use.

ERIC A. MACDONALD

Eric MacDonald is the newly appointed International Counsel for Graydon Holding, NV and holds the position of the Director of New Products and Market Development at Graydon America. Mr. MacDonald is an attorney by profession specializing in international business. Originally from Canada, he received his BA from McGill University in Montreal and his law degree from Osgoode Hall in Toronto.

Prior to his arrival at Graydon, Eric was employed by Imperial Oil of Canada and the law firm of Blake, Cassels & Graydon in Toronto. Eric advises on American and developing market credit industry issues and on multi-jurisdictional legal matters. In New York, he spends his time developing new export related products including country analysis profiles, internet applications and educational seminars and also oversees the market research development at Graydon. Mr. MacDonald has written a book on Latin American credit guarantees, has published many articles on global credit and business topics in American credit related magazines and trade journals and frequently speaks on international credit related issues throughout the U.S.